RADIANT DAYS

RADIANT DAYS

{a novel}

MICHAEL A. FITZGERALD

SHOEMAKER & HOARD

Library of Congress Cataloging-in-Publication Data

FitzGerald, Michael A.
  Radiant days : a novel / Michael A. FitzGerald.
    p. cm.
  ISBN-13: 978-1-59376-131-8
  ISBN-10: 1-59376-131-7
  1. Europe, Eastern—Fiction. I. Title.

PS3606.I884R34 2007
813'.6—dc22

2006030692

Cover design by Kimberly Glyder Design
Interior design by Megan Cooney
Printed in the United States of America

Shoemaker & Hoard
An Imprint of Avalon Publishing Group, Inc.
 1400 65th Street, Suite 250
Emeryville, CA 94608
AVALON Distributed by Publishers Group West

10 9 8 7 6 5 4 3 2 1

For Catherine

RADIANT DAYS

{ PART ONE }

Why on Earth would anyone make anyone in one's own image?
—Martin Coreless-Smith, *Nota*

{ one }

MARSH ASKED ME to join him on the veranda for a cigarette. He didn't look like a war correspondent. He had pale skin, a cherubic face, and crimson pouty lips. He wore his thinning blond hair swept back. He smelled faintly of week-old milk. I took a bottle of cheap Russian champagne from the kitchen counter and followed him out.

The brunch had been going since 10:00 AM, and now dusk was beginning to fall. Drinking all day had given the air a blurry effervescence. I leaned over the flimsy cast-iron balustrade and could see the Virgin Records sign beginning to glow red over Kossuth Ter. The clicking of trolleys and tinny honking of the Trabants below drowned out the voices back inside. To the west the sun was a lonely smoldering star, balancing on the horizon. Its rays sheared from under the low, rust-colored clouds, reaching between the silhouetted buildings that capped the hills across the river in Buda like fingers trying to hold on. My cheeks ached from smiling so much.

I asked who was winning the war.

"Chaps with guns," he said, lighting his cigarette. Then he grinned and nodded toward Gisela, who was speaking with a Peace Corps person. "Where did you pick Pocahontas up?"

His eyes were on her behind. She was wearing tight black pants that stopped at her calves and flared above her black boots. Under a thin cotton crepe blouse, you could make out her bra. "San Francisco," I said. "We met there."

"But she's Magyar, isn't she?"

"She's been living in America for a while. This is her first time back."

"She's lovely," he said.

"Yeah," I said.

"And native enough to bum out the Yankee gals." None of the American women except Ellie had been particularly friendly to Gisela, but she intimidated the men as well. "Poor enlightened feminists," he continued. "Your American colleges ruin them. Have them playing field hockey and all freaked out about pronoun usage." His gaze left Gisela and fell upon the half-dozen other people still drinking. "They've no chance against the natives," he said.

"I like her."

"You should," he said, "but is it really necessary to bring them to the parties?" Then he laughed. "How long are you in town for anyway?"

I shrugged. "A few weeks. We'll see how it goes with her son." I had told him our situation.

He nodded and turned back to the cityscape. The last bit of sunlight was hitting the poplars that lined the boulevard below, and their pistachio leaves shimmered under an imperceptible wind.

"What do you do for work?" he asked.

"Web programming," I said. "But I'm not sure anymore. We've just been here a few days. There seem to be teaching jobs?"

He nodded. "There's a crucial difference between tourists and real expats," he finally said. "And it has nothing to do with whether they have a job or not."

I waited.

"Real expats carry their porn with them," he said, smiling. "Buying new magazines in each new city is too lonely and expensive."

"I guess I'm a tourist then," I said. I had never heard anyone described as an expat until that week. He was probably the first British person I'd ever spoken to.

Marsh was wearing a leather Gestapo coat and a red silk scarf. He had graduated from Oxford a year before. Earlier in the day, he had recited a poem about champagne by Browning. I wasn't sure whether to believe him, but he said he was covering the Balkan War for London's *Telegraph* and that he just kept an apartment here in Budapest for recreational purposes. There was no way I'd ever met him before, but still, he seemed familiar, like maybe he'd been on television or played a minor part in a movie. And later on, in the months after he was killed, it sometimes irked me that I had never asked him about this.

My cigarette was finished and I waited to see what he was going to do with his. There were smudged ashes on the railing, but no actual butts on the balcony. I thought maybe they came back inside with us, but then he flicked his out over the street. It arced through the dusk haze and made a small fountain of sparks in the wake of a tram. Mine followed, landing uneventfully on the sidewalk.

He turned and said, "You know, you should just make it up. Create yourself. No one will stop you. That's what they all do." He nodded into the living room. "It's refreshing. As Mum would say, like dousing your tampon with club soda." Then he slapped me on the shoulder. "You should be a sculptor."

"Club soda?"

"Or make movies. Or open an English-language bookstore. Or a bar, and let know-it-alls like me drink and pontificate for free. It doesn't matter. Any American in Budapest is here because they were losers back home. Just make it up. You can do anything. It'll be better than what you were doing." He nodded into the living room. "These expats," he said sarcastically. He held up his glass and silently cheered them. "What wankers. Like they suddenly 'became' something by getting on a plane. Get an f-ing life." He took his coat off. Sweat stained the underarms of his oxford. "They call the U.S. 'the States' like it's some quaint little place that they know all about. When most of these people haven't wandered too far from a few major cities in New England, northern California, or the small town of their private college." He smiled. "And of course, the patch of national forest their NOLS class dropped them in." His cheeks were turning a flaring pinkish red, and his green eyes had become glassy and mostly pupil. The rest of his face was still pallid and damp.

"The only real barometers of Budapest that expats should care about are the price of Russian champagne and whether the students are still willing to sleep with their English tutors," he said, but with less conviction, like it was an often-repeated idea that might not have been his. Then he looked up: "There's some equation, isn't there? The amount of sex, the quality of the fucking, being in direct proportion to the distance, east or west, you are from Omaha? There's something like that, isn't there?"

I shook my head and shrugged. My champagne drunk was starting to go limp.

He held up his glass again, this time waiting for mine: "Oh, fuck it," he said and smiled. "Cheers."

I followed him back into the living room where people were sitting on a buttery velour couch and lying on a large sisal rug. Gisela looked up as Marsh and I entered. She waited for the Peace Corps person to finish some observation of Hungarian culture then excused herself and came over. When she got to us, she brushed up against me and lightly tugged on one of my fingers. I hadn't gotten used to her beauty yet. She was

Magyar but looked almost Middle Eastern. Her eyes were brown and striated with lines of aqua, and there was an ashen quality to the skin around them. Her nose was long but delicate. She had her henna-tinted hair up in a barrette and downy wisps curled loosely off her thin neck. I reached around her and placed my hand on the small of her back.

People had been eating all day but the table was still lined with food. Little bowls of caviar. Blue-veined creamy cheeses. Soufflés. Two roasted chickens. An asparagus quiche sprinkled with paprika. Orange juice. Fresh vegetables. Brie and pears. A Thai peanut butter and cucumber angel hair pasta. Bottles and bottles of fifty-cent Russian champagne— whenever we ran out, someone would collect change and walk down to the ABC and buy a few more. There was a fruit salad containing slices of kiwis, peaches, bananas, grapes, and pineapples, fruits I had never seen for sale in the small grocers'. A tray of deviled eggs. A small side table of alcohols: Bombay Sapphire gin, Absolut vodka, French white wines, Eger reds.

Warm damp drafts drifted in from the terrace.

". . . What else is there to do?" a boy in a seersucker suit, who was in vet school here because he couldn't get into one in the U.S., was asking the room. "Where would you rather be? It's cheap, it's beautiful, it's centrally located. Paris is a three-hour flight. Greece, two. If the Hungarians would stop letting their dogs shit all over the sidewalks and we could get NPR, Budapest would be perfect."

"But it's not real," a small blond woman answered. "There is a world turning without us. Back in New York and L.A. things are happening. We are definitely not 'paying our dues.'"

"You think temping at some shitty corporate job makes you a better person? You think you would be more human, feel more deeply, if you had to pay twelve hundred dollars a month in rent? It's so obvious what is wrong with majoring in finance, working at Merrill

Lynch, or going to law school. No intelligent person actually does that anymore."

"Yes, they do. You're just too much of a spoiled nitwit to know those people. There are millions of Americans who just want a safe nice life. Kids in Boise, in Albany. Everyone in this room had an exceptional childhood. But if you hadn't, you'd want money. You'd major in finance."

A dramatically handsome guy stood from the couch. His facial features were perfectly symmetrical and his skin unblemished. He hadn't spoken since we arrived. For most of the day I had assumed from his silence he was drunk or Swiss, but on the veranda Marsh told me he was an American filmmaker and that his name was Todd Verlaine. He had grown up with Richard Linklater and been involved in the movie *Slacker* and had come over with Linklater to shoot *Before Sunrise* in Vienna, but quit halfway through and moved to Budapest to make a film he and some college friends wrote. "I had a bad childhood," he said. "A real shitbag childhood." Then he held his hands up, shrugged, and walked into the kitchen.

The seersucker vet student raised his eyebrows, waited for someone to say something, then continued. "Maybe," he said to the blond girl. "But I think the America you're talking about has become so well-off that even those kids are bored with money, with buying shit. That is why advertisers go after younger and younger age groups. No adult in America can, in good conscience, walk into a mall. Everyone, poor or rich, knows that malls are a joke, a symbol of what is wrong with our culture."

"You are so completely out of touch."

"You're so completely condescending to middle-class America."

Ellie walked in from a side room where coke or something was going on. She had changed. She was now wearing a silk kimono and slippers, with chopsticks poking out of her dark curly hair. As she crossed the room, stepping over the people who were draped across the floor, she gave us the heavy metal, Devil-horns sign. When she got to us, she hugged Gisela and then me.

"You're having a good time?" she asked.

I gave her a thumbs-up. She was the host. She had approached Gisela and me in a café the day before and, I assumed, because she heard us speaking English, invited us to this brunch, which she held every Sunday.

"As I was saying"—still the seersucker guy—"there is nothing for Americans to do, to feel. No history. No faith. No struggle. We point and click our way through wars, jobs, life. Everything is so nothing. We have no causes. Could you imagine being a hippie or protesting things? Even if I hate everything, it's all just so nice. So easy. I have no choice but to be happy. I'd be a complete fake if I was angry.

"Even when I drink hard or get druggy for a while, I can't fuck up my life. I will always have a job or grad school. I will always have a place to sleep. Fuck, I will even always have someone to sleep with. It is so nothing. All of this. All of us. We are so nothing. Not just people in Budapest or Prague, but everywhere. We aren't slackers anymore. We are just soulless well-dressed nothings. Perfect consumers. Clean, healthy, traveled, educated nothings."

Marsh leaned across me to Gisela and asked, "How do you say 'shut your fucking pie-hole' in Hungarian?" Gisela smiled and obliged him.

He laughed and offered her his hand, almost wedging me aside. "Marsh Mathison," he said. "It's lovely to meet you."

She let him take her hand.

"Anthony tells me you've lost your son?"

"Did he?" She gave me a quick look.

"Not to make light of it, but how does one go about doing that, losing a child?"

"Painfully."

He stopped smiling. "I could help you," he said. "I've spent some time with the various departments, directors, institutions, the quagmire that is the Hungarian government."

"That's nice, but no thank you."

"If he looks anything like you, he may already be in America. Americans have been over here combing the orphanages for Caucasian babies since '89."

She sucked on her top lip with impatience.

"Sincerely, I'd be glad to help. Have you been to Pécs? There must be a hundred thousand orphans down there, streaming in from Bosnia."

"My son's Hungarian."

"Right, but I *know* people is what I'm saying. People who know about the state institutions. A good friend of mine, Charlie. I could—"

"Really, thanks but no."

He shrugged. "Well, take my card." He pressed it into her hand. "And if you need any help. . . ." He drained his champagne. "Cheers." He walked off to fill up another glass.

"Margaret has genital warts," Todd Verlaine said as he walked back into the room with a glass bowl of beets, walnuts, celery, and gorgonzola. It looked like a bowl of guts. "Margaret isn't healthy. Genital warts can lead to ovarian cancer, which can lead to an emotional, sad death, which seems to be something real."

"What the fuck are you talking about?" Margaret shrieked. She was Ellie's roommate, a tall redheaded girl from Atlanta who was the account manager for Purina Hungary. Earlier she told a story regarding a recent focus group where an old man stopped his dog and helped himself. She'd also been whining all day about an ongoing PR crisis involving black marketers who shipped Puppy Chow to the Ukraine for human consumption.

"Someone said we aren't real? I heard you had warts," he said. "And if you could get it, I'm sure the rest of us probably can. Shit, six degrees? All I'm saying is that we probably aren't *that* healthy, so maybe that makes us *something* instead of *nothing*."

"I do not have fucking warts."

"'Fucking warts.' That's funny. Get it? 'Fucking warts.'"

"Who are you? Who invited you?"

"You did. I'm Todd. We kissed a little bit the other night at Tilos az A."

"No, we didn't."

"Yeah, we did. And you know, it's kind of a social responsibility to tell us what the deal really is?" He put the beet salad on the table and began pouring himself a mimosa. "Sex happens so randomly now and we all drink so much. I bet Americans in Budapest have their very own strains of some of these viruses. Some version of chlamydia that smokes a lot and is bent on travel; it has a perfectly good host body, but has heard through a friend about some other great body that's really cheap and might be worth checking out."

"I do not have warts. I don't have anything. I can't believe I'm having this conversation. Please leave."

"I'm not done yet." He took the mimosa to his lips.

Then the seersucker guy said, "Well, the Hungarians should at least do something about the dog shit." Someone agreed and said that they thought you could download NPR off the Internet. It seemed totally acceptable that Todd wouldn't leave the party. It seemed for that day, you could do anything.

❈ ❈ ❈

On the tram home, an hour or so later, Gisela wouldn't look at me. She was staring out the window, holding the bar on the seat in front of us so tightly her knuckles were baby-skin pink. A warm rain had begun falling as we were leaving Ellie's.

"Why did you tell that man about my son?" she asked.

"He wanted to know what I was doing here."

Her eyes reflected in the tram window, staring hard at nothing. Past her image, the glass was blurry with spidering rivulets and drips.

"It's none of his business."

"What do I tell people?"

"Tell them we are in love. Tell them you love me. You followed me over here. People will like that."

"People will think I'm a sap."

"What, Anthony? We aren't in love?"

Is there a *Teen Vogue* article that is required reading for every fifteen-year-old girl? Are they taken aside the moment their breasts start to bud and told, "No man knows his heart. No man knows what he really wants or what he should say or do about anything having to do with love, even in jest. Just say it confidently and you will always be in charge." I wasn't in love. I didn't know how I felt, but she was the most gorgeous woman I'd ever touched and my heart was speeding. I swallowed. I reached across her and put my hand against the drips on the window. She lifted her hand from the bar and placed it on my thigh. She smiled, waiting for me to calm.

"My nice guy," she finally said. She stretched up and kissed my cheek. Then hugged herself against my arm and whispered, "My body feels alone."

The tram went along the inky black Danube. She eventually let go of my arm and pointed up at lights at the top of the hill on the other side. "Gellért and the Castle District." She pressed her finger against the window and drew a line in the condensation. "The tower on top of the hill used to be a monument. It was the last place to fall to the Nazis. I think it is a disco now, run by the Mafia. And the Castle is a mediocre art museum. They've got a few of Picasso's plates."

The tram turned back into the city. Shops were closing. Salamis and shanks of prosciutto hung in deli windows like torpedoes. There was a statue in the middle of a traffic circle of a man holding a musket, looking vaguely like Lenin. The red awnings over the café patios were dark with the drizzling rain. A wet billboard with women diving into azure pools took up one whole side of a building. Another had waiters holding out platters of bursting, impossibly large foods. Four-century-old churches moped in the shadows of newer skyscrapers. A McDonald's glowered from a building older than the United States. We passed a courthouse with a floodlight illuminating an embossed mural on its wall. The mural depicted healthy, squared-jawed farmers and factory workers staring off into a radiant future. The men and women had shoulders and chests like superheroes and were surrounded by a bounty of wheat and grapes.

The tram stopped and more people got off than on, then it continued down the wide boulevard until it cut into City Park. There was an empty Ferris wheel, a cold-looking merry-go-round with shiny wet horses, and a boarded-up, green-roofed concession stand. Rain, like machine-gun spray, fell on a small dark lake.

"You see that pond?" she asked.

I nodded.

"It was home to a dozen swans until Romanians ate them."

{two}

Two weeks before, in San Francisco, paying my dues, I had cowered through a day, hungover and useless, hiding in my cube until around four-thirty when I decided I had been miserable enough all day to be paid for it and slinked out the door by the mailroom.

My plan was to go straight home and eat a half-pound of steamed broccoli, tear my closet apart until I found my rarely used Asics, and begin a new life as a jogger. (I also would scheme on how to never set eyes on Claire Murphy again.) But as I got off BART at 24th Street, the sky had begun to darken and the wind was picking up. I decided one pint of beer wouldn't kill me. I walked down Valencia towards the Lone Palm.

At that point, I wouldn't have been able to find Hungary on a map. I didn't know you spelled it with an "a." I didn't know Croatia was its own country. I knew there had been "fighting" in Yugoslavia, but didn't know what it was about. I imagined something like Northern Ireland: home-made bombs, ski masks in July, hunger strikes. I had never once thought about or said the phrase "Hungarian orphans."

Gisela was behind the bar, looking like she subsisted on Marlboros and Diet Coke. I don't know how I knew she was Hungarian. It was something everyone knew, but no one knew what to do with. She had worked at the Lone Palm for over a year. She and I had never spoken outside of me ordering drinks. Generally she seemed furious, delivering every drink with a complete and aggressive lack of interest in you, anything you've ever done, could possibly do, say, or think.

But that night it was different. She said hi as soon as I walked in. I wasn't ready for this and air went down the wrong pipe. I tried to suppress my cough. I nodded. I smiled. I worked my way onto a stool at the end of the bar.

"You're just coming from work?"

I nodded again and uh-huh'd, then said nothing and started fishing around in my blazer pocket for matches. Before I found any, she slid a pack of the Lone Palm matches across the black Formica top of the bar. She asked what I was drinking.

"A beer."

She raised her eyebrows.

"A Hefeweizen," I said.

"You need a lemon?"

"Sure," I said, not caring either way, only vaguely aware that I would agree to anything she suggested.

She walked down to the beer taps in the middle of the bar. She pulled a frosted glass from the refrigerator and poured the beer. From where I sat, I could see her whole body. And it was all great. The perfect flatness between her stomach and where her thighs pressed forward. Long thin calves. Her butt wrapped in a short black skirt. I tried not to stare, but it seemed part of the service. She leaned forward and the hem of the skirt rose above her muscular thigh, flirting at the curve of her ass. She tapped her right foot nervously to an unheard music. Looking at this foot, I noticed her shoelaces had a few small knots where the string had broken and been tied back together. This struck me as an incredibly sad thing on someone with such a life-affirming behind.

When she returned with the beer and a coaster, she told me the beer was on her and asked if I knew that in Hungary they called lemons oranges.

I didn't.

"These here," she held up a slice of lemon from the small cutting board. "They are called 'Magyar Narancs.' It means 'Hungarian Orange.'"

"What do they call oranges?"

"We don't have oranges. Just lemons. I grew up thinking that lemons are what the rest of the world thought of when they said oranges. The Russians originally promised us all schoolchildren would have an orange every day, but when things didn't work out, they handed out lemons."

"Then what were your lemons?"

"I don't remember," she said. "Limes? Maybe apples. Good question." She walked away and tallied some things on the pad next to the cash register. I started on my beer. I let the first gulp tingle in my mouth before I swallowed. After it was down, I sighed. My vision sharpened. The ache in my lower back dissipated. I sat up straighter and cracked my shoulders. Everything settled. I eyed the piano. All the crap from the night before began to wash away. Then she looked up from her pad and asked me what I did for a job.

I told her about CNET. I told her I worked with a bunch of other Web people who, like me, supposedly "made" websites.

This was San Francisco 1995. It has since become clear we didn't do anything. Because of all the money being thrown around, there was the vague feeling that sitting there in our quasi-technical-sounding jobs we might be doing something—it seemed impossible Wall Street was so wrong about us—but at night, when you stood in your twenty-five-hundred-dollar-a-month studio, looking at yourself in your full-length mirror, you thought, "What did I do today? Who paid me?" And the answers were pretty obvious: "Nothing." And, "Someone who got completely ripped off."

I hadn't meant to get the job. It wasn't Plan A. It wasn't Plan B, C, or D. I had moved to San Francisco in 1993 with Claire directly after college with Beatish hopes of working in a liquor store and writing novels. But that was before the Internet. There were no jobs, even in liquor stores. After a year of working a long and unimpressive line of shitty temp positions, accruing massive credit card debt, and lowering my literary aims from novels to maybe a short story here or there, I became a producer for CNET. A friend's girlfriend got me the job. I was at the Unexamined Life one night having The Debate—whether Oakland was the new Mission—with my friend's girlfriend. And the next thing I knew I was "a producer" for an Internet company. The job title sounded real—my mom said "the producer" instead of "a producer," like I was in charge of putting together the sequel to *Gone with the Wind* instead of the Top Ten Modems list for October's issue—but I have no idea how I actually filled my days. I didn't have a single technical skill to speak of. I told the girl this. She said it didn't matter. And it didn't. I couldn't type. I didn't know what a browser was. I had never been on the Internet. I didn't have the vaguest idea how it worked. Why you would want to use it. But she told me to not talk much and watch what other people did. Other people seemed to sit in their cubicles emailing each other to see if they wanted to walk over to South Park for a latte.

I remember on the first day realizing you could play music CDs in the computer's CD-ROM drive and thinking that was cool.

I was supposed to be the organizer of the editorial and the technical people, but both parties knew their jobs better than I did and I spent most of the time—over a year—listening to CDs, trying to look busy while staying out of the editorial and technical people's way, and surfing the up-and-coming Web in the ongoing contest with my friends to uncover the most gruesome porn site (the original Butthunger.com). This was all terrifying for the first two months but after a while I got used to it and came to assume that this was what everyone did. I even got used to the money. I was salaried at fifty-two thousand dollars a year. Before that I had been making eight dollars an hour as a temp. It was completely mind-blowing—nearly two thousand dollars every two weeks. Everything became easy and light. I took cabs everywhere. I ate out every meal. Claire and I flew to Cabo a few times on whims for the weekend. I joined a gym I never used. I bought a four-hundred-dollar set of knives. I went in on a ski house at Lake Tahoe with people who made me hate that I was white and American.

Any capable person who showed up in San Francisco after 1994 with artistic aspirations was ruined. There were simply too many jobs. If you could draw a straight line in sand, you were hired on as an interface designer. All the would-be painters became graphic designers. The writers found themselves "developing" content. Anyone who had an AOL account before 1995 could hire themselves out as an Internet consultant (or "insultant," as they were called). There were literally thousands of these job titles that hadn't existed before 1993 and none of them meant anything. People quickly learned that if they could keep the buzzwords changing, the people over thirty would be thinking that we knew something that they were too old to learn. Portal. Goofering. Netizen. Push Technology. Hypertext. Just dumb-ass fluff jargon created by twenty-three-year-olds to make it seem like they had ideas that the people who had money didn't. It wasn't even geek speak, just goofy shit people made up while sitting around South Park—fifteen minutes before some meeting, eating their focaccia-bread sandwiches—as a way to explain what they had been doing all month. And then once the new buzzword was out there, they were paid crazy amounts of money to try to implement it.

"It's an okay job," I told Gisela. "My father likes it. He likes the health insurance. My mom too. She likes telling her friends I work for an Internet company. She says one of our generational gaps is the difference in the meaning of V.C. For her it meant Viet Cong."

"Will you quit this job that your mom and dad like?" Gisela asked.

"I don't know. Even if they didn't like it, I've gotten used to the money."

"What if you didn't need money?"

"What if I was a capable heart surgeon?"

"In Hungary you don't need money. Everything is cheap there. This beer here," she pointed to my glass. "Fifty cents. Food, apartments, everything is cheap. With five thousand dollars, you could live for a year. They even have real oranges now."

"I thought this beer was free?"

"Do not joke. It's very nice. You would like it. Believe me, Hungarians are an interesting people, lonely and sad, isolated by their language. And it's inexpensive. And the women are very very pretty."

"You're from there?" I asked, instantly embarrassed.

She paused. "I left seven years ago." Then paused again, counting to herself that it had been that many years. "But I'm returning in two days for a visit."

"Why?"

She considered her hands. "To get my Mikos," she said, "my son."

"Son?" Like it was a species I had never heard of.

"I haven't seen him since a few days after he was born."

"Oh," I said. She looked back down and slowly shook her head. After a silent moment, she asked and I told her my name.

Then she said, "It is a very sad story, Anthony."

I nodded contemplatively and made some throat noises, but inside, my stomach flittered from hearing her say my name.

"My father was a bad man," she said. "He left my mother when we were little. My mother had no one. No money. No family. Hungary back then was very hard. In order to get along, she had to do things that would make anyone crazy."

I nodded some more.

"My mother cracked up. We were taken away after she tried to drown Akos in a public fountain. We went to a Catholic orphanage. We wore winter coats inside all year. The nuns had no money and were unhappy because of the Russians. Everyone worked, even us children. And the nuns were not good people. Two of them used to touch one another. They'd take some of us girls and make us watch."

I laughed.

"My life is a joke to you?"

"No, no, it's not that."

"Maybe you think it's funny that when I was fifteen a man from the village got me pregnant? I was forced to give up my son. Funny, no?"

"I wasn't laughing at you." But something in her freaking out was comforting; a small chip in her personality kind of leveled the playing field.

"In 1988 I was selected to go on an exchange program to Cleveland for the summer. From there, I ran away. Originally to Chicago, but eventually here. And now I pour drinks for rich people who whine about the fact that their jobs are too easy."

"I guess be happy you aren't pouring drinks for poor people who whine about foreigners taking all their jobs."

"I don't know where my mother or son are. I don't know if they are alive. I've lost my baby."

I took another sip of the beer, careful not to greedily chug it, and then slowly set the pint glass down on the bar. I fixed on the bubbles in the glass rising and, for a second, had the disorienting feeling that instead of the bubbles rising, the glass was falling. I stopped looking and picked up my cigarettes. "I'm sorry," I said and tapped the bottom of the pack until one popped halfway out. I had read somewhere recently that we're more resilient to our childhoods than they used to think but I didn't say anything. I offered her a cigarette. She looked at it and then me and laughed.

She stepped back from the bar to catch her breath. The headlights from a car turning the corner swooped through the room. She illuminated and then darkened. "I got a letter from my older brother, Istvan, last month," she finally said. "It was the first I have heard from him. He is now a grown-up, living in Budapest, and I am going to see him. He says that we can find my Mikos."

I wished her luck, but she didn't respond. She turned and walked back to the center of the long bar, dragging her rag along the countertop, then stopped at the beer taps and just stared at the drips coming from one of the spouts. A near minute of silence. Her humor gone, fixated on the dripping tap. I don't know. Despite what she ended up doing to me, I honestly believe she felt bad before we even left for Hungary.

She started nodding like she had come to a conclusion. "You're a nice guy," she said, then turned away and pulled a pint glass from a red dish rack and started drying it with a faded yellow towel she kept tucked into the waist of her skirt.

Every time I was about to finish one, she deposited another beer in front of me. I thought that as long as I was only drinking beer, I'd still be in okay shape to start the jogging in the morning. And just when I was drunk enough that I felt I had something intelligent to say about her life, intelligent enough to wow her into sleeping with me, I caught myself, dropped a twenty on the bar, and walked out.

❁ ❁ ❁

An evening fog had rolled in. Little herds of people walked from restaurant to bar to bar. Taxis unloaded Marina chumps who slummed it in the Mission for a few hours every Friday and Saturday night. Halos of illuminated mist hung around the streetlights. Lonely and self-righteous in my loneliness, I needed to continue drinking, to really bottom out before I could start jogging and turn my life around. I went over to the Latin American, but it had recently become a hot spot among members of what Claire called "the Brylcreem Drill Team" and was packed with idiots in zoot suits and girls with pigtails and knee socks. I had one Jim Beam-and-water and left. I thought about going over to Claire's but wasn't quite drunk enough. I walked to Taqueria Cancun on 19th and Mission, thinking I should eat something, but the line was too long. An hour after I left, I found myself back in front of the Lone Palm.

It wasn't too crowded yet. My seat at the end of the bar was empty. But the patrons were drunk, and there was something rambunctious in the air. People were laughing and talking loudly, being smug, being young and alive, smashed. And I wasn't. All the men in the bar looked like this dick at work who always referred to me as "Bud." I was too sober to start a fight.

Gisela seemed to have her hands full with a neighborhood homeless guy, Green Man. He was telling her the Lone Palm needed more houseplants, but then, realizing he wasn't in a house, he started saying that the place needed more barplants. Then he went off on a riff about bars growing on trees. When he saw me watching him, he asked if I'd heard about

Mayor Willie Brown's secret proposal to turn Candlestick Park into a holding pen for homeless people once the 3M ball field was complete. I said I hadn't. "It's cold out there," he said.

She smiled when I ordered a beer and asked if I had missed her. I couldn't tell if she thought it was creepy I came back.

As I drank the beer, my chest balled up and I came close to crying. I'd open my mouth but couldn't pull air in. I wondered if telling Gisela about Claire and what happened in the kitchen would lead to some sympathy sex.

I ordered a shot of Jim Beam and put money on the counter, but again she didn't charge. This relaxed me some. I sipped the shot, waiting for the alcohol to cloud over my loneliness. I ordered another shot and drank it straight down. It was like water. I felt it in my throat for a second but then the warm blur racing through my body that usually followed, didn't. I couldn't go back to my apartment sober even though Asher had promised me he wasn't going to "date" Claire. But I couldn't just sit at the Lone Palm all night and accept free drinks.

Gisela worked the bar, enduring jokey drunk guys. I thought of Claire and what Asher and I had done. I tried to picture Gisela with a bag over her head on my kitchen floor. She was too taut. Her little black T-shirt revealed a tight, strong tummy, and women with bellies like that don't get walk-around-naked drunk. They are not victims. Then I tried to imagine someone doing that to my sister, Tara. I'd kill that someone. I'd bite his cheeks off. I would have him picking his teeth off the floor with broken fingers. I pictured my first-grade teacher, Ms. Pendleton: gray slacks, a white blouse, shoes with a little bit of heel, a red sweater tied over her shoulders—kind of seventies preppy—and a Wegman's grocery bag over her head. My mom: ankle-length jean skirt, white turtleneck, a silver chain necklace on top of the turtleneck, a crisp brown bag over her head. My

Grandma Tara, my sister's namesake, her head in a shopping bag. A mental black-and-white: my grandmother as a young girl dressed in one of those old-fashioned full-piece bathing suits that cover everything. There was a Ferris wheel behind her. She was at Coney Island or some beachy amusement park. She had her hands on her hips. Her stance was forward. She was proud. Just off the boat. She didn't even seem to notice the bag. It was like someone had told her this was the newest style. A bag on your head was just part of the American Experience. I realized I could categorize all women by whether I could picture them with a bag over their head or not. Those I could, I wouldn't sleep with while sober.

While I was thinking this, Gisela stopped mid-pour and walked down the galley way. I was gazing at her, but not really conscious of it until she was directly in front of me and then I was suddenly embarrassed.

"Will you come to Budapest?" she asked. "With me?"

"What?"

"Come to Budapest with me."

I let the phrase float across the ticker-tape of my mind. . . . *With me. Come to Budapest with me. Come to Buda.* . . . It was the nicest thing anyone had ever said to me. It was better than getting into college. I shrugged, trying not to freak out. I looked down at my beer, nodding slowly, as if beautiful women requesting my company on an international jaunt was a daily occurrence.

"Why me?"

She thought about it and shook her head, smiling. "None of my present boyfriends would."

"Persuasive."

"I don't mean you look stupid, you just look nice. Like a nice guy."

"Ouch."

"You look like a nice guy who needs a vacation."

"I'm broke." I had just started a 401(k) and was doing that weird crap: the ski house in Tahoe, the gym membership.

"Okay," she said, nodding. She walked away and left me alone for the rest of the night except to occasionally drop off another beer. When I was getting up to leave, I asked for the tab and she handed me a napkin: *372-8347 = Far away + Gisela.* She held the note in my hand for a second and looked into my eyes. She leaned across the bar and put her lips on my mouth. We stayed there. Her mouth widened. She pushed her tongue in and traced along the inside of my teeth. She pulled back an inch and bit into my lower lip. Her breath curled around my ears and neck. She let out a slight moan, then released my lip and slid back behind the bar.

"I leave in two days," she said. "You should come. Your mother could tell her friends you went to Hungary with a beautiful stranger."

I folded the napkin and stuffed it into my wallet. My mom would say, "He's in Europe working for a Catholic charity. Helping the former Communists." My mother who still calls nearly every Sunday afternoon and asks how mass went that morning.

❀❀❀

I got under the covers. The kiss, the beer, and the damp evening air left me chilly inside and excited. I held my breath, shivering. Fuck Asher and his new girlfriend. That was a beautiful gorgeous kiss. That was real. *Come to Budapest with me.* It sounded like a thing, a thing you could tell your children. *When I lived in Budapest.* My life had become silly. A job my mom liked. Cabo. And until recently, a girlfriend my mom liked. My highest aspiration: to jog.

I started to set the alarm clock and then stopped myself. I put my hand down my boxers and rubbed, but despite the kiss couldn't get anything to happen. In the morning, I'd blow off work. Mary Ziegler would need to put together May's Top Ten Modems list all by herself. I had around thirteen hundred dollars in my checking account. I'd buy Gisela some new shoelaces and spend the day in the travel section at A Clean Well-Lighted Place.

I read for a bit but kept getting distracted by the sound of someone rooting around in the Dumpster below my window. Eventually I passed out, the book on my chest. Sometime in the middle of the night, I woke and turned off the bedside lamp.

{three}

A HIGH SANDSTONE WALL surrounded St. Eszter's Home For Children. The rain had stopped during the night and now the heavy damp spring wind was blustering at the thin new leaves. Small blossoms from a dogwood tree shook loose and collected in rings around the evaporating puddles. When the air gusted, all the noises got drowned out, and then, seconds later, the wind would cease, and shrills of the playing children would fill in around us as if we were in the middle of their games. A soccer ball arched into view then dropped back down below the wall.

A woman wearing a blue lunch-lady smock answered when we rang the bell on the gate. She and Gisela talked, then she led us inside the pale lime-green building. She showed us down a hall to some chairs outside an office and asked us to wait. A young boy with a harelip stuck his head over the glass window of a classroom door. I waved. He smiled and ducked back under.

My idea of an orphanage was basically Oliver Twist, gruel and burlap shirts, but these kids seemed happy. We could clearly hear the rustle of joy. Doors opening and slamming shut. Children erupting from rooms in games of tag. The sharp clear sound of kid voices, even in another language, discussing kid issues. A baby would begin to cry, setting off a string of other crying babies until they seemed to tire themselves out and then the lead baby would start again. Like geese flying, one taking the lead, then dropping back after it tired. Out in the courtyard, the soccer ball pinballed from one kid to another.

Gisela lit up a cigarette.

I gave her a look.

"You should probably smoke too," she said. "You'll seem more Hungarian."

"Why can't we just look him up?" I asked. "Why aren't you sure of where he is?" She had told me we were scouting St. Eszter's, posing as prospective parents.

"They cannot tell the birth mother. But Istvan has friends from when we were kids, kids who never got adopted and now work for the children's services. They think he's here."

"This is the best way to go about this?"

"It will work. Just be my nice guy."

Then there were footsteps and American voices. A couple in their thirties was following the blue smock lady down the hall toward us. The man dressed in pressed khakis and a blue V-neck sweater. The woman wore Levi's, pumps, and a little pea-green raincoat. They were normal-looking Americans, but in this shabby setting they looked moneyed and spa-buffed. When they got to us, the attendant swept her hand at the two empty seats against the opposite wall. The American guy kind of half-bowed to the lady and said, *"Kosenem sapien."* The woman also said "Thank you" in English and touched the lady's shoulder. They sat down and shyly smiled over at us.

"Hey," I said.

"You're American!" they both immediately chimed.

"Yeah," I said.

"Oh, hi. So are we."

"Yep," I nodded and looked at Gisela who was chewing on a cuticle of the hand that held her cigarette.

The guy stood and leaned across the hall with his hand out, "Mike Kimball, and this is Lucy. It's so nice to meet you, see some friendly faces." I stood and shook his hand and met Lucy half-way and shook her hand too. I pointed to Gisela: "Gisela." She looked up and smiled and kind of waved. Then we all sat back down.

"It's heartbreaking, isn't it?" Lucy said.

I smiled and nodded, trying to demonstrate some seriousness.

"How long have you been 'in country'?" Mike asked.

"A few days," I said.

"A few days? Count your lucky stars. We've been here for eight weeks, and we are just now getting inside, just met the kids on Thursday. Got the run-around for a while, but things finally seem to be going smoothly."

"She's Hungarian," I said, pointing to Gisela.

"Oh, inside track then, lucky duck."

"Yeah, I guess."

"Have you met your someone special yet?" Lucy asked.

"Not yet," I said.

"We met one special little guy, but then we met another and another and then little Stephan. Four little miracles!"

"Four?"

"Well, we fell flat-out in love, and I mean in love, L-O-V-E love, with little Gyula. We fell hard. But then, god bless him, he went and had two older sisters and a baby brother. The sisters didn't live here and had never even met little Stephan. But they came out for cocoa with us yesterday, the whole lot, and they're just sweeter than honey. Just glorious. Angels."

"And you're bringing them all back," I said. "Four children?"

"Yeah, sometimes you can't guide by logic," Mike said. "You've got to follow the heart." He took his hand up to his heart and pat-patted.

The director, a meticulously and sternly dressed woman in her fifties, opened the office door and, speaking in English, invited Gisela and me in.

Mike gave me a thumbs-up. I smiled and crossed my fingers.

The director was wearing an ironed gray skirt with a stretchy matching coat. She had a white skunk stripe in her black hair that was taut in a short ponytail. Her large breasts were piled up in her brassiere, but her nipples were pronounced like a young woman's. The breasts looked really warm. I stared and then didn't. I put my hand through my hair. I put my hands in my pockets. After we sat, I felt myself tighten in the crotch. I crossed my legs. I looked at the walls. I stood up and pulled on the front of my pants. I sat back down. She hadn't stopped smiling. I couldn't tell if the smile was the face she wore when she was enduring someone or if she was really happy. Despite her breasts, she didn't seem like a naturally happy person.

"So you are looking for ein kinder? America's all out?"

"I'm Hungarian," Gisela answered curtly. "You should have gotten our papers?"

"No, no papers yet," the woman answered, but continued beaming. I had never heard of "papers" before.

Then they ditched me, bantering back and forth in Hungarian for about twenty minutes, occasionally stopping to explain for my sake that Hungarian children aren't like Asian children or even Romanian children. Did I know those children are often dumped by the roadside? Foreigners come in and buy those children. Women are having babies to sell to American organizations. The Romanians are starving. But this is not so with Hungary. Hungarians are Catholic, the patriots are; the Communists were never able to take their faith away.

Hungarian orphans are usually from smart, happy women who just had babies while they were too young. Because of their faith, they know not to waste a baby's life. And although our circumstances, mine and Gisela's, weren't frowned upon, Hungarian orphans are much more likely to be adopted by people from their own country than, say, Romanian orphans.

Eventually Gisela pulled a folder of papers from her shoulder bag. "These are copies, but you can see they have the correct stamps."

The woman took the folder, opened it, and read for a few minutes, occasionally shaking her head. She turned to me, "You like Hungary? You think you'll be okay with a Hungarian son?"

"Hungary's great," I said. Gisela gently pulled her cheek to my arm. I smiled down at her. My natural ego was taking over. I wanted to win the prize, wanted this woman to like me and give us a kid.

"You don't think he'll be lonely in America?"

"It's a melting pot, no one's lonely in America," I said.

The woman nodded and looked back at the papers. She picked one up and held it to the light for a minute, then slipped it back into the folder.

"They're just copies," Gisela said. "The originals were sent by post."

She tapped the folder against the desk. Sunlight from a high square window stretched across the wall behind her. "Don't insult me," she finally said.

"No one's insulting anyone."

"I will talk to the authorities," she said. "Who do you work for? What you're doing is not legal."

I stood. Gisela remained seated and ripped into her in Hungarian. Then they were both yelling in Hungarian. Gisela stood and sat back down again. The woman stood and pointed out the door. I started for the door. Gisela stood again. She grabbed at the folder on the desk. The woman yanked it to her chest. With her free arm she remained pointing toward the door.

Gisela pulled a letter-size envelope from her bag. "You know there are better places for them," she said holding the envelope toward the woman.

The woman looked at the envelope, then Gisela. *"Nem,"* she said. No.

Mike and Lucy pretended to be discussing some practical details of their angels being delivered as we walked past.

❖ ❖ ❖

We got off the tram in the city center and walked down some steps into a basement bodega. I took a seat at the far end of the bar, slightly outside the main circle of light, and ordered a beer while Gisela went into the WC.

She came out and put some coins in the pool table. As we played, dust particles, like schools of little fish, floated and swirled in the shafts of daylight that reached in every time someone opened the door to the outside. The bartender seemed annoyed we were playing. He looked up when the balls clacked loudly and pushed his sleeves back to display forearms covered with thick hair.

"That was not good," she said.

"Did you try to bribe her?"

"This should be easy," she said. "They should want people to have their children back."

I took my shot. "Is there more to this? I can't get arrested."

"It's fine," she said. "That woman was just a little whacked-out."

"She seemed to think we were breaking a law."

"She's just a bureaucrat. She hates the world. We're not doing anything illegal."

"Okay, but let's be sure, if possible. I can't get arrested."

Gisela smiled and stuck out her tongue.

This cheered me for a moment, but a few beers later, I felt weepy. Things seemed out of my control. I wanted drinking during daylight hours to bring us somewhere. I wanted her body lonely again. "What are we doing tonight?"

"Something fun," she said. "To make up for that mean lady."

"Will it cost money?"

"Have you ever done opium?"

"Yeah, I think so, maybe once."

"It's Turkish. Makes a yummy tea."

The apartment we were staying in overlooked the Danube on the Buda side. It felt like I was being ferried there secretly. Sneaking past guards. Our cab crossed the Szabadság Bridge, and there was still some blue in the sky, but the lights of the Castle were on, and they glowed in the humidity of the evening. Gisela sat up front, giving directions, and I was in back with the windows down, letting my body sway and roll like seaweed as the driver navigated the narrow streets of Buda. At our apartment building, he pulled up onto the sidewalk. The old woman in the ground-floor flat shamelessly watched us through the grates of her windows as we got out and slowly walked into the courtyard with the pear tree. The voices of neighbors came from the apartments above. Pigeons cooed. The elevator creaked and moaned its way to the third floor.

Inside I flopped onto the couch and had to concentrate to keep from blacking out while she boiled water in the kitchen. She told me Istvan had given her the opium, which for some reason made me jealous, but I was into the tea aspect. I had smoked opium in college; there was a semester when it was everywhere. And I had had mushroom tea a bunch of times. Although mushroom tea is a different thing, the tea aspect was always appealing, gave a healthy spin to something that might fuck up your genetic structure.

She came back in with a tray and served the tea in a miniature set of china. The small flashes before my eyes stopped and I could breathe again. From the floor-to-ceiling window in the living room, we watched massive rain clouds billow north of the city. The sky darkened and thunder crackled and boomed for ten minutes before the rain started. The windows were open, and once the rain began, air vacuumed through the apartment, rustling the posters on the walls and sending papers from the desk across the room towards the windows. She had Glenn Gould's *Goldberg Variations* playing, and we drank cup after cup of the sugary black tea.

I was being eaten by the old leather couch. I couldn't get enough of it to touch my skin. I had both my arms spread out across the back and with each inch more of couch a warm tingle would swell through my head and chest.

She was standing at the window looking back out on the Danube, the heavy drapes next to her shifting in the gusts.

"During the Revolution," she said, "the Russians and our security police, the AHV, threw students' bodies into the river."

I tried to stand but couldn't.

"Towards the end of World War II, when the Russian troops moved in to liberate the city, the Germans poured the dead Jews and Gypsies into the water, hoping to hide what they had done. Three hundred thousand bodies. The river was so thick with corpses you could walk from one side to the other. But look at it now. It's so beautiful, isn't it?"

I needed her to know that I liked her and that was all. "People can't really express 'like,'" I said. "A simile, a distrust of reality, of love. You don't need sex to fuck everything up, just 'liking' a person is enough.

Because it's obvious that everyone wants to have sex with everyone. Sex has become ubiquitous. It's no longer part of anything personal, it's the norm. And sex doesn't really mess things up; actually truly liking someone is where the freakout begins," I said.

"Jerry Garcia died today," she said. "It was in the papers." She was still looking out onto the river and city. She held her right hand up over her shoulder and gave the peace sign.

"We'll find Mikos," I said. "We can do anything. I know we can. I'll help you. In any way I can, because I 'like' you. No strings attached. Not love. Not 'want to fuck' but 'like and want you to have everything.'" With every ounce of my being, I managed to stand up. "Walk around me."

She turned from the window. "What?"

"Walk around me."

"Walk around you?"

"Haven't you ever seen that movie?"

"I don't think so."

"Humphrey Bogart asks Lauren Bacall in *To Have and Have Not* to walk around him. Just do it."

She came across the room. "Like this?" she asked.

"Yep."

When she finished, I said, "I like having you around."

"You're really high."

"Yeah. . . ." I clenched and unclenched my hands, like I was priming myself. "But still my world is a better place when you're around."

"You're going to feel silly in the morning."

"The world is a better place because of things people feel silly about in the morning."

"That's one opinion."

"Can we go to bed?" I asked and pulled at her finger. We hadn't kissed since San Francisco—I'd been sleeping on the Murphy bed.

She moved into me and put her hands around my waist. Her mouth touched my neck and stayed there. She bit softly, then stopped and sucked. Then she whispered: "We have to talk."

When is that ever good? "Okay," I said but pulled her closer.

"No," she said. "Really, I have a confession." She pulled her arms up between us.

"I'm sure it's all right."

She looked down at her hands and I kissed her forehead.

"Whatever it is, we'll figure it out."

"There's no Mikos," she said. "I don't have a son."

My mind cast around for her motives for having lied to me, or more particularly whether these motives would get in the way of me sleeping with her in the next few minutes.

"I work for a group in California, All God's Children," she said. "I get kids out of Hungary, and sometimes Romania. About twice a year, I come over and bring them back to the States. For money. AGC got me out. I was older, but they saved me."

"Is it legal?" But I was also kind of thrilled by her confession. No longer a single mom, and now she owed me.

"Another matter of opinion," she said. "There's a bureaucracy. Those people today were right. In the last few years it's gotten worse. Since '93. Some things happened involving organized crime, mostly the Russian mafia, essentially slavery, and the sex trade."

She looked down toward my abdomen and pulled her hands up to my chest. "It's okay," I said, patting her hair. "It's all right. We'll figure it out."

"But you shouldn't be here. I shouldn't have lied to you."

She let me pull her closer. I kissed her forehead again. "Seriously, it's cool," I said. "It's fine. I'm psyched I'm here."

She shook her head.

"I'm totally psyched to be here. I don't care you don't have a son."

"Yeah, I can see that," she said.

Finally in bed, I held myself above her and after she undid my belt and the buttons on my jeans, she nimbly lifted her feet up, hooked her toes into my pants and pulled them down to my ankles. I kicked them off from there by myself. Then my shirt was over my head and I was between her legs. Her feet locked behind me, her heels encouraging.

The opium had me sad-happy enough to stay for a while and although she made noises like she was coming, when I finally caught my breath, my shoulder was wet with her tears.

Afterwards she walked out into the kitchen naked, uncorked a bottle of red wine and took some chocolate from the refrigerator. She came back in with a large chunk already in her mouth. She handed me a piece. I tried to get it to dissolve in my mouth with the wine. I wondered if I would remember this as our first or our last.

"What are you really like?" she asked, sitting down on the bed.

"What do you mean?"

"You're different than you look, in bed."

"Size matters," I said.

"You better hope not," she answered and smiled, rubbed the covers above my groin. Then she raked both hands through her hair. "No, you just look like you'd feel one way, but then felt different."

"Different 'good'?"

"Yeah. Different."

"So you thought I was going to be bad."

"No, just another way."

She looked at her hands and the floor, then stood. She pulled on her white panties and beige silk chemise and went into the living room, leaving the two French doors open. She sat at the small secretary and started drawing on a pad.

"That journalist was going to Pécs?" she asked without looking up.

"There's some U.S. base there," I said. "Taszár or something. He claims the U.S. trains Croatian soldiers and sends them back to fight the Serbs. He also said there was a refugee camp. Full of people fleeing the war."

"That man liked himself. Found himself very interesting."

"I liked him. He was pretty funny."

"Did you like how he looked at me?"

"He can look all he wants."

She smiled and puckered her lips, then kissed the air. I lay back. My skin was alive. I closed my eyes and moved my hands down along my abdomen. It was still wet with sex. I moved my hands further and pulled it around some.

I woke before midnight. The windows were open. I wasn't wearing any socks and the bottoms of my feet felt iced. Gisela was sitting at her desk doodling. I watched her for a bit, trying to telepathically get her to come back to the bedroom. Then pulled the covers back and padded over.

"Hey."

She put her arms over the drawing and laid her head down.

"You all right?"

She nodded.

"What are you feeling?"

"Want," she said.

Underneath her thin arm, I could see half a detailed pencil drawing of a young boy. I stood there for a minute, touching her hair, and trying to make out more of the drawing. She had given him large eyes and jagged dark hair. The stillness of everything began to feel heavy and I lifted my hand from her hair and walked back to the bed.

✿❀✿

We were secured away in this high-ceilinged apartment with the crazy view of the river. She told me about her childhood, her family breaking up, her brothers Akos and Istvan. She said lying to me had been spontaneous. She never thought I'd actually agree to come. And now she felt bad. She showered me with gentlenesses. She showed me the city: the bathhouses; bullet holes in the buildings of District VIII where students had been shot in the beginning of the '56 uprising; the Roman ruins in the suburbs of Buda; the red marble monument to Raoul Wallenberg, a Swedish playboy who gave up his life trying to save Jews during the war; the National Museum, where a whole wing was dedicated to paprika, Hungary's beloved, and arguably only, spice—a special favorite after Albert Szent-Györgyi was awarded Hungary's first Nobel prize for discovering vitamin C via it; the Heroes' Park where they'd herded all the Soviet-era statues together in a single park and you could buy marzipan figurines of Lenin. To take a break from the lard and meat, we ate at the Hare Krishna center in Buda, the only place in town you could get vegetarian. We spent mornings in the elegant cafés and, at Grundel one night, she ordered pigeon soup, which she said tasted like park: cigarette butts, old men, and discarded newspapers.

It was spring in Budapest. People weren't going home after work. The cafés stayed full. Women test-drove summer dresses and skirts. Skin was everywhere. Men shaved. The flowerbeds on Margritsziget, an island in the Danube, were bright. Expats were always out on an open lawn behind the ruins of a church playing Ultimate. Running around like dogs. A bunch of Embassy workers and English teachers, dudes in ponytails. Kind of knowing they looked like dinks, but thinking they were being true to some idea of Americana by not conforming to the Hungarian idea that anything besides smoking, drinking, sex, and reading is a waste of time. The horse chestnut trees that lined Andrassy Ut going out to Heroes' Square were dense with budding deep-green leaves. After a day of walking around and eating, Gisela and I would sneak back up into the amazing apartment and have sex and walk around naked. There was an ancient claw-footed tub in the kitchen. We took baths together where she showed me the trick of tooth-picking a tin full of smoked oysters and letting them float in the tub with you while you lazily ate them. Once during a bath, I told a story I had told her before about my childhood dog, Pooch, who used to chase the dog catcher's truck, and she said we shouldn't feel it is necessary to always talk. She said a famous Hungarian poet once remarked that all conversation can be boiled down to two things: "I love you." Or, "Now is not a good time."

On the night before she left, I had a sex dream about Marsh. I can't explain why. He had more or less repulsed me at the brunch. So sweaty and pale. He looked like a baby who hadn't gotten older with time, just larger. Plus the milk-smell.

The dream began as a pretty normal dream; something was chasing me and I was running down a green hill, which resembled Song Mountain, the ski resort I grew up skiing at, during the summer and somehow ended up at Marsh's house or he was chasing me and was going to kill me and then we suddenly became friends.

His dick looked like a regular dick while he was approaching me but then it peeled back like a banana being peeled, only there was no banana underneath. The inside of the skin was fleshy and pink like a vagina only instead of halved down the center, the four fleshy peels formed a flower with four tight pink petals. And we didn't have full-on sex, I just stuck it into his inside-out, peeled-back dick and came immediately.

I woke up wet and lay perfectly still, wondering if I'd made any noise and how I was going to get the cum off my belly. There wasn't a washing machine in the apartment. I listened for Gisela's breathing. For a long while there was nothing, but then she exhaled. She was awake. I stayed still and waited. It began to puddle on the inside of my hipbone and then slowly leak off onto the sheet. I quietly moved my hand down to my side to dam it up.

Finally her breathing became regular and I inched up on my elbows. A car passed in the distance. Her breathing stayed steady. I rubbed what was in my hand around on my belly and carefully stood and silently wiped it off with a sock. I lay back down and listened to her breath and thought about getting up for a glass of water but didn't and this went on for an hour or so until I was asleep too.

At dawn she was up and walking around. Half asleep, I listened to her gently open and close drawers. I remember thinking it was nice she was trying to be quiet. I vaguely remember thinking I heard her go out the front door and that I'd soon have hard poppy-seed rolls and butter.

When I woke for good, the sun was up and the air in the bedroom was hot and parched. She wasn't next to me. I slipped from bed and walked out into the living room. It was empty and still, and I felt as if there wasn't enough oxygen. I opened a window and the breeze gave me the shivers. I wanted a cigarette. I took a deep breath. I said her name. I said, "I think I'm gay." I laughed kind of maniacally. I tried to remember if Claire ever said anything about talking in my sleep. I went into the kitchen and wet a washcloth and wiped off the crusty film. A key sat on the kitchen table. I reheated and drank the espresso on the stove. I went back to the bedroom and got dressed. I found my cigarettes and went out the door. I thought about smoking on the balcony but changed my mind and walked over to the elevator, which had a pale layer of condensation on its iron gates. As I descended it struck me this was the first time I'd been out of the apartment on my own.

In the street the air was pearly with morning sunlight hitting the remains of the cool night fog. I pulled out a cigarette and stood around smoking, hoping she'd appear. After a second cigarette, I slowly began to walk. I eventually went left, then left, then left. Then I went right, right, and then right. There was a gusty morning breeze and it almost felt like fall rather than late spring. I couldn't see the river, but I decided if I followed the cold I'd eventually reach it. I walked for over an hour. Children were traveling in bunches to school. Workers in blue overalls sat at the Bierstubes, small wooden huts shaped like kegs, drinking the morning ritual of Nescafé and beer. It was chilly in the shadows, but between the buildings, the sun cut through and was drying the dew from the streets. I turned a corner and found myself standing on the banks of the slow-moving Danube. The rising sun played across the dark water like silver rope. I followed the river north along the western bank towards the Margit Híd. They don't maximize the riverfront in Budapest. It isn't like Florence or Paris, built around its river. The Danube is wide, probably a half mile. There are very few cafés or shops. Expensive hotels rise at its edges like cliffs. And the Parliament building, and the occasional old woman selling completely random shit: a pair of shoes, two bananas, an English issue of *Sports Illustrated* from the late 1980s, some bras hanging from her arm like gutted fish.

I began to feel faint and headed home.

A note was on her bed stand. It was on the same stationery she had used to draw the picture of the little boy. It must have been there when I first woke.

Anthony,

I'll be back in two weeks, maybe three. Do not leave. I just need to take care of some things. It's been nice. I miss you already. I'm missing you right now, and now, and now.

Love,
G.

{four}

Dᴜʀɪɴɢ ᴍʏ ᴛᴡᴏ ʏᴇᴀʀꜱ in San Francisco, I had written thirty-two pages of My Novel. It was about a musical movement where bands purposefully contracted terminal diseases. Some bands injected themselves with AIDS, smallpox, and yellow fever and then died, along with their music, slow pitiful deaths. But one band, The Dogs, locked themselves in a garage with a rabid raccoon. They wrestled around with the animal until it sunk its teeth into their flesh. The whole band contracted rabies and soon became rabid. Their shows got better and better. They became animals. Raging. Feverish guitar. The lead singer howling. Until they died.

I had never played in a band. I didn't have any musical friends. I can play the theme to *Star Wars* on the piano. I didn't go to very many shows.

I spent those first twenty-four hours of Gisela's departure skulking around the apartment, going through drawers. In the front hall closet there were some men's suits made of heavy wool. I tried them on. The waists were big enough for two of me and they smelled like smoke and urine. There were yellowed receipts in the top bureau drawer, but nothing else. In the medicine cabinet I found an ancient pair of horn-rimmed eyeglasses.

I had credit cards but no way to pay that month's minimum. I had spent most of the original thousand acting like a big shot and paying for everything and I now had about fifty U.S. dollars left.

On the second day, I read the copy of *Jesus' Son* I'd brought with me. I read it over the course of the afternoon, each story successively. When I was finished, I reboiled some opium that she left in a tea ball, and read it again. His sentences were so easy. Poetry but not esoteric. Transcendental but graspable. They hopped right up in your lap. He made genius look easy. I decided I was going to make my genius look easy too. I started compiling a list of titles and ideas for my second novel.

By day three I started getting on a "writing" schedule: wake around nine, masturbate, read in bed until noon, masturbate, go have a pastry and coffee, walk across City Park to the Szechenyi bathhouse. Do some laps in the pool as old men played chess on the floating chess boards. Then have a salami and hard roll sandwich for lunch, maybe a beer. Stop at the American Library to read the *Economist, Harper's,* and the *New Yorker,* and return and check out books.

In the library one day I discovered Marsh was a bona fide journalist. His byline was in the *Herald Tribune* attached to a large piece about a bridge in Bosnia that had been blown up after surviving for four hundred years.

After the library came what I considered my one deviation (from what was really a long list of deviations): on the walk home, I'd lean against a wall outside a grammar school a few buildings down from ours to watch the moms pick up their children.

The school was in an old dark-gray building, its entrance two large wooden doors. When both doors were open, a car could drive through. But there was also a person-sized door within one of the large doors,

like a pet door but for humans. The first day I ever walked by the school
I noticed a group of women standing around in the chilly graying
dusk, breathing mist like a small herd of horses on a cold dew-covered
morning, talking among themselves, getting on with the business of
mothering. They all looked so practical. Occasional smiles, but only for a
careful instant. Comfortable warm three-quarter-length coats. Nothing
immodest that would make them seem any different from the other
mothers and embarrass their children. Some were younger than others,
but none were what you would call "young women." They were a bunch
of Hungarian moms.

Then there was the rustle of children's voices behind the heavy
doors, and the mothers hushed and turned to see the sharp colors of
the small coats spilling out onto the sidewalk. Ten-year-old boys holding
hands, hugging and patting each other on the backs like aged war heroes.
*Csókolom. Szia Zolt. Hallo, Hallo. Csókolom, Anya, Csókolom. Szia Mikos. Szia
Andras.* And little skirts twirled as red-cheeked girls looked round and
round for their mothers' expectant faces. And they ran in small saddle-
shoed steps into kisses and warm hands that quickly straightened collars
and pulled wool hats down tighter over nearly wet eyes. Little strange
voices bouncing off one another in an awkward choral symphony, the
adult voice with its wide breath and, even better, children's voices:
prickly natural sounds, natural and singular like the wicked sound of a
fish jumping on a still lake. And the mother and child pair off for a second to tell one another how good it is that they are both together again,
and then look back at their friends and say good-bye one last time and
hug and trade double-cheeked kisses and then move off—small hands
wrapped in the warm long womanly fingers—into the early evening
and faint glow of the first lit storefronts. Such a huge moment of almost
inexplicable happiness in a daily routine. Then I went home and boiled
some potatoes.

The library books were classics I was sure I had read, except I hadn't: Faulkner, Fitzgerald, Hemingway, Joyce, and some Russians. I bought a used copy of *The Red and the Black* because Hemingway said it was essential, but I didn't open it once. I read the first ten pages of the *Swann's Way* and the first fifty of *Brothers Karamazov.* I couldn't get past the opening two pages of *The Sound and the Fury,* because I grew up next to a golf course and am too hyperactive to ever be good at golf and have come to despise the sport. I did get through most of Fitzgerald and Hemingway, though. In fact I read *A Movable Feast* twice. And I read their biographies. Finally I read the short stories of Raymond Carver and Tobias Wolff. They had both taught at the Syracuse MFA program and, in the back of my mind, I was considering letting the program have a look at my stories and drafts of novels when I finally wrote them.

When it had become apparent she was really gone, I began to venture out to the bars. I never felt like I was going in the right direction until I stepped around a corner and spotted the line of people in front of an entrance. (In the mornings, there was the suspicion that the bar from the night before was an irretrievable mirage that would be gone if I went again to find it.) But inside, the air was dense with smoke. I'd steer away from the *langos:* crepes they stuffed with anything: chicken livers, chocolate sauce, ketchup, anything. I'd look through the tables full of expat guys wearing business suits, the badge that you weren't a ubiquitous English tutor. Even if I only had enough money for three beers, I would have one as soon as I got in the bar. I would sit, smoking, trying to look both content and distracted, and I'd have little contests with myself about how long I could make the beer last. I would sometimes gulp and then slowly let the beer slip from my mouth back into the glass. The beer was generally served warm, so it didn't matter how long I took to drink it. I'd sometimes look up and stare at the people I felt were the least likely for me to stare at, like big guys or the most unattractive woman in a group of women. After I finished my first beer I would move around the bar, pretending to be looking for someone. I would sometimes believe I had a preordained date. A friend. Ellie. Someone who wanted to give me a job that I wouldn't take. I'd walk around the crowd looking—for a split second—at each table of people, just long enough so that anyone at the table who noticed me could tell that in less than a second I was able to surmise no one at that table could possibly be the person I was trying to find.

There was something about the expat bars that was too easy. They were the cheeseburger of living abroad. Easy because everyone speaks your language, because people looked hip but not as alienatingly hip as in, say, any club in New York or San Francisco, and because compared to the same kind of club anywhere in America, they were cheap. But they were painful because, just by walking through a door, you went from being a foreigner, the ultimate loner, the man looking in, to being an expat, a member of a phylum that in Fitzgerald and Hemingway novels meant vapid hang-about. The worst type of expat bar clientele actually called themselves expats, members of the expat community, the people Marsh loathed. Budapest had a bunch of these places: Picasso Point, Paris-Texas, Made Inn, Tilos az A (which was Hungarian for the TRESPASSERS W sign in *Winnie-the-Pooh*; the woman who told me this wore the information like a badge), and others that weren't exclusive to expats, but where only expats could afford to go every night of the week. I told myself I was different because I was starving and couldn't really afford the fifty-cent beers. I sat there with my warm beer-slash-spittle, wincing at the world around me.

On one of the first days, I found a Robert Mapplethorpe exhibit at a gallery owned by Yoko Ono on Fő Utca. There were self-portraits besides the whips and orifices. One in particular of him lying on his back in some jeans, taut and stretched across the floor, was really inspiring. I couldn't get it out of my head. That was what I wanted my body to look like. Wire. String. Heroin, 1978. I got a little carried away.

I pretty much stopped eating. For three days, I tried to live on vitamins alone. I had been carrying them around in my dopp kit since my
mother gave them to me when I first left for college, five years before. It
seemed like a great idea. Just getting the good stuff. Each morning I took
one horse pill–sized multivitamin on an empty stomach, then reeled
through the rest of the day dizzy and faint. My body ringing with weakness. On the third night of vitamins-only, I woke drenched in sweat. My
body vibrating from the violent *thunk-thunking* of my heart. So I added
one or two potatoes, some caffeine, and more beer. By the beginning of
the second week, everything felt tight. Like I had been working out, only
I was probably the weakest I had ever been.

Since in its essence starving is less of something, it should free up
more time to do other things. This wasn't the case: starving took all day.
To make it less painful, you need to break the day up into small increments
and get through each increment without eating. You can skip breakfast by
remaining in bed and masturbating. Though if successful, masturbating
results in a net loss, so it's ideal to just sleep. In fact, starving almost
demands sleeping in. If you get to 10:00 AM, you can take a long bath,
spend some time in front of the mirror, bothering a pimple through the
lunch hour. Then read until 2:00 or 3:00, which will be your "work" part
of the day. Then get out of the house and walk or watch people or go to
the library, and once it starts getting dark and the wind picks up, slowly
plod home. The egg and heel of bread waiting for you will be ten times
better than if you'd eaten them that morning.

Bread, eggs, and potatoes were the staple foods of my starva-
tion. They cost just a few cents and could be bought from any of the
small ABCs.

I had a lot of time to get creative with potatoes. I baked, mashed, and
fried them. Fruits and vegetables weren't readily available, so I would
crush up vitamins with the potatoes. Potatoes and vitamin C. Potatoes

and calcium. Sometimes I splurged and spent what amounted to seventy-nine cents in forints on vegetables at the Wendy's on Oktogon Ter where they put tomatoes and lettuce on their cheeseburgers.

By the end of my second week, my ribs were showing. My desk-job paunch didn't really shrink; it just turned rock-hard. And with the loss of cellulite, my body began to eat itself. The calories it was burning were much higher quality glucose. You feel faint for the first three days, then your body and brain go into overdrive. It is like being on a sugar high all the time. Only no nausea. You sweat easily but you zoom. And with the big empty apartment, I beat off constantly. Little balls of tissue began to herd around the bed. When I wasn't beating off, I did sit-ups or attempted to write.

It was probably just the poor diet, but slowly an ashen feathery sadness began to cover everything. Dark things moved just beyond the periphery of my vision. I was being watched. I'd find myself standing on the sidewalk bawling, unsure how I'd gotten there. The apartment suddenly felt haunted. Dreams became increasingly vivid and they would take place in the apartment. Sometimes in the middle of a sultry afternoon a cool draft would blow through the streets and it would seem no one else would notice the temperature change. I'd feel the wind, but flags wouldn't lift, leaves stayed still. The bright trees and clothes began to seem papery and if I looked at them too hard, they would tear and crumble. The world was fragile in a way it hadn't been before. I felt the need to tiptoe. I had the general suspicion that the big solid things were made of water, that buildings were about to splash to the ground, that tramcars could at any moment dissolve and we, the riders, would find ourselves wet and abandoned in a puddle in the middle of the *korut*. On an elemental level, I felt that the core of everything was dark and water.

I began to suspect I wasn't getting enough oxygen. Despite all the flowers and budding trees, there was no getting around the pollution.

Gray acrid exhaust poured from the cars. On the edge of the city, thin smokestacks bore black smoke into the sky. Everyone smoked cigarettes. Myself more than ever. When I wasn't smoking, I tried to think about my breathing. While out in the streets, I made a conscious effort not to breathe deeply. On the trams, where I thought the air was somewhat cleaner, I'd inhale deeply, visibly, to the dismay of the other passengers, like I'd just emerged from a lake. I flared my nostrils to allow for more air before I went back out into the streets. I thought maybe my nasal cavities were too boogery from the pollution, so I was constantly picking or blowing my nose. When I was on poorer streets or places where I didn't think I would run into many young women, I wore a white dust mask.

Making genius look easy was a pain in the ass, so I quit My Second Novel and started trying short stories. I wrote the first two pages of about six. Then I decided letters might be a better way to get the juices flowing. I sent one to my parents telling them I was in Hungary and okay. The rest went to people who shared the unfortunate luck of both being in my address book and being, at one time, on the receiving end of rude behavior by me: ex-girlfriends; almost-girlfriends; a Penelope Arthur—in care of her parents—who in seventh grade I regularly referred to as "pizza face" and taunted with some nonsensical joke about her use of Clearasil and whether we "should sue the company"; a priest at St. Mary's who my mother had sicced on me during a turbulent year in high school. Long, long letters meant to make amends, to show my newfound maturity and thoughtfulness, but that succeeded only in telling a few people, who for the most part had forgotten or wished they could forget me, that I was starving in Budapest. To this day, I feel a little awkward knowing these cries for help are still out there.

❀ ❀ ❀

Todd Verlaine, the filmmaker, was sitting on a bench in Kossuth Ter. When he saw me, he waved. This was surprising. I hadn't seen him outside of Ellie's brunch and we hadn't spoken that day except to be introduced. I walked over. His mouth was full. He motioned for me to sit down.

"Budapest is made out of concrete," he said once he finished swallowing. "The communists tried to rebuild it after World War II, but they substituted concrete for granite and now because of the shoddy building materials the buildings all look much older than they really are." He was eating an apple strudel. His mouth was messy with bits of walnuts and cinnamon.

"I didn't know that," I said.

"Ironically, as a result of its decrepitude, the town has a second life as a Hollywood set. There are tons of movies being made here. Hollywood likes it because it's cheap and looks like a city stuck in the fifties. Madonna's movie *Evita* was filmed here last year. The 1995 Budapest is the stand-in for a 1950s Buenos Aires."

We hadn't yet said hello.

"Do you get satellite TV?" he asked.

"I don't have regular TV." I hadn't seen a television outside the hotel lobbies and some of the expat bars. And the only channel you could get in English was Sky MTV.

"I've got a dish rigged to the top of our place; it's usually good for one hundred and forty to two hundred channels."

Then I remembered overhearing one night of a fabled American who became everyone's best friend during the Super Bowl, World Series, and NBA finals.

"And this morning, at around 4:00 AM, I was watching *Triple X Talk* on New York public access. Have you ever seen it?"

I hadn't.

"It's not porn, it's a talk show about porn. Every week they have a sex topic and interview various and sundry sex industry people. But they don't actually have sex on the TV. For example, last night the topic was 'Sex Toys': blow-up dolls, Ben-Wa balls, whips and chains and dildos. And they have porn stars, Dr. Ruth wanna-be's, retail people, et cetera. . . talking about this like it's a serious topic of discussion."

I laughed.

"And after a while they field questions from the audience and take phone calls from people out in television land like you and me."

"You called in?"

"No, jackass, but . . . well, first I gotta tell you this side story. . . . I'm from Texas, but went to Berkeley and my senior year some buddies from home came out to visit. And we did what you do with friends from home, let them insult your new college friends and then drink until you can disillusion yourself into liking them again. And we somehow ended up over in the Tenderloin and somehow ended up in a porn shop. We were just fucking around, asking consumer-type questions about Sex Glitter and cock rings, just stupid drunk shit, and after we finally walked out of the place, my friend Louis pulled this huge dildo from his overcoat. He had stolen a thirty-six-inch dildo called the Anal Destroyer."

"Three feet long?"

"The size of a baseball bat. It was fucking lethal." He held his fist out in front of him, like a nineteenth-century boxer.

"Anyway, we just fooled around with it for a while. Smacking each other with it. Trying to get it in our mouths and whatnot, and then he must have put it in his coat, because I don't remember seeing it for the rest of the night, and then the next day they left and I never heard about the Anal Destroyer again . . . until last night."

He waited for me to ask. "Last night?"

"Yeah"—he was laughing—"I'm fucking watching *Triple X Talk* and they have people on saying the usual bullshit about liberating puritanical America though vibrators and penile graphs and shit and then they take a few phone calls and they get this one from a woman in Texas, and immediately I recognize her voice. I couldn't quite place it at first, I just knew that I knew that voice. And then she starts going off about her boyfriend and how he came home from visiting a buddy of his in California a few years back with a huge dildo and that it was the best thing that ever happened to their relationship. He used it on her, and she used it on him, and it was just the greatest thing. She wanted to give dildos two big thumbs-up. And by now I completely recognized her voice; it was definitely Louis's ho girlfriend, Beth.

"So I immediately call Louis. It was 3:00 AM Budapest time, so it was still only about 8:00 PM in Houston. Anyway, the fucker wouldn't answer the phone. I got his machine and I'm like, 'Louis, it's me, Todd, calling from Budapest, and buddy, I just wanted to tell you that Beth just told the whole fucking world via transatlantic satellite that she dildos your ass. And that you love it. You love the Anal Destroyer. Way to go, man. Two big thumbs-up for dildos!'"

His eyes watered. He put his hand through his unkempt hair. His laughter turned into a cough. As he shook with the coughing, breadcrumbs loosened from his sweater and fell to the ground where pigeons would soon be on them.

❈ ❈ ❈

On the way back from the baths one day, I sat and rested on a bench by Parliament. It was at the top of the large stone steps that descended into the moving whiskey-brown water. Old bent men stood at the bottom steps and fished with long thick bamboo poles. They smoked and talked, occasionally testing their lines or rebaiting their hooks with fish entrails. They didn't seem too serious about catching anything. Most of them sat close to each other, sharing *palinka* and cigarettes. The water was shiny with an oily film, and I couldn't imagine eating anything pulled from the polluted darkness. Then as I was about to leave, they began cheering and one of them, walking backwards, like he had something too big to just reel in, pulled a massive carp—as thick as a football—up onto the steps. A boot went down on its head until the fish stopped moving. A man held the line tightly, pulling and pushing it like a stuck gear, eventually tearing the hook from the fish's mouth. Instead of pitching the bottom feeder back into the moving water, the man kissed the fish and raised it up to the sun. Water ran off it in strings. Then he pulled a chain bearing a dozen or so other carp from the water and threaded the metal through its gills. They were fishing for polluted carp. A democratic move, but disgusting to my Copper-River-salmon-and-Point-Reyes-oysters sensibilities. After a round of congratulations, they went back to it.

I looked across the water and then up into the hills of Buda. The Castle sat low and wide like a giant brown bullfrog. The city was dirty; even on the river you could smell the choking diesel exhaust. A linty gray filth covered the corners of the buildings next to stop signs. The men ate carp from a polluted river. But I had written more in the last two weeks than in the rest of my entire lifetime. I was really really skinny. I didn't speak a word of Hungarian. Gisela was who knows where, but I had slept with someone so beautiful and exotic and might someday again. I had this crazy big apartment all to myself. And Budapest—its blustery third-ratedness. Maybe the pollution made it seem more human than a Paris or a Rome? It wasn't Vienna, the other city on the Danube, a city I Eurorailed through during that semester abroad and had reminded me of a hospital or a really clean mall. The Hungarian language was so difficult that there wasn't even the possibility of going native. The people were still a little sheepish after thirty years of Communism. Less confident. Things were dirty, imperfect. I was off everyone's radar. My parents would just have to tell their friends "He's living in Hungary." Just getting by could be an occupation. I could write home about the exoticness of going out to buy a peach. Maybe really write a book, finish something for once in my life. Maybe I could ask for a credit increase from Visa. Go to operas, which might bridge the huge divide between my father and me. I'd be out of San Francisco and everybody's cheesy contentment with themselves and their stupid dotcom jobs. At the very least, I could put off having to ex-plain myself for a while longer.

Then, as I was standing, ready to move on, with my hands in my blazer pockets, I saw Marsh walking with a young woman. It had been almost three weeks since the brunch. He was wearing red jeans, his three-quarter-length leather coat, and a white scarf. The woman looked young, maybe a teenager. They were walking side by side. Coming up the river from the south. Her dark hair was combed straight. She had slim delicate hands and wrists. Her face was narrow with thin groomed eyebrows and pensive lines on her forehead. She had a hard upturned nose and fine carved lips that were red with lipstick and, although she wasn't talking, lively. She was carrying a cheap black vinyl attaché case that seemed too large for whatever her needs might be. And wearing a thin cream rayon sweater that had a sparkly quality and a purple mini-skirt and was clumsily trying to navigate down the sidewalk in spiky high heels. She looked like she was going to interview for a secretarial job at a small failing business. He was leaning into her, talking fever-ishly. I couldn't hear him but she nodding slowly as he yapped away. His fervor and her reserve made it seem possible they didn't even know each other.

Her beauty and Slavic features couldn't cloak that she was pitiable, hopelessly poor, but she was somewhat saved by a visible awareness that this was just a stage she was going through. This was an outfit she had to wear at least once, though she knew it wasn't how she was going to be for the rest of her life.

Now she was giggling at what he was saying; doing that thing women can do for about three months of their lives when they are between youth and womanhood. Both completely aware of his intentions but still able to feign innocence. Her eyes wide open, surprised, but her mouth a tight red smirk. You can talk and talk but what this is really about has been obvious since minute one.

The way they walked so closely. The next natural step would have been for him to put his arm around her. The way she instinctively knew it was about sex. An unabashed "Yep, people do it. That's what this is about." The way, I thought, he was shamelessly pursuing someone too young, someone whose real personality was probably veiled behind a foreign language.

Like someone clapped his hands in front of my face, that obnoxious dude who lives in the back of your head: HEY! This is it! This is why you should be in Hungary! You can chat up a woman, a girl, so outside of your life, so exotic and young, so poor. This is a place to behave badly. A place to do what you couldn't and wouldn't. Such a contrast to the uptight PC-ness of San Francisco.

Suddenly they were walking back towards me. He waved. I felt my face flush, remembering the dream.

"Anthony?"

"Hey."

"What are you doing?"

"Just walking around. These guys just caught a massive carp."

"Something other than fisherman," he said. "I'm still thinking sculptor."

"I can't believe they would eat them. The river seems filthy."

"I don't know," he said. "Babette? Do they eat the fat bottom feed-ers?" She smiled shyly and nodded.

"Anthony, this is Babette," he said.

I double-cheek kissed her as I'd seen everyone do in the bars.

"She's a pianist," he said laughing. "She's brilliant."

"Cool," I said.

"Anthony is a sculptor," he said, but when I didn't laugh, he stopped. "So how are you? How's Gisela?"

"I'm okay. Kind of out of it. Gisela went somewhere."

"Like her son?"

"She took off. I don't know where. Left a note saying she'd be back, but she's not yet."

"Hmm."

"Yeah," I said.

"But you're staying in her place?"

"It's not hers. She rented it."

"But it's nice?"

"Incredible, it's huge. Just right over there," and I pointed across the river, a little to the north. "About three blocks in from the river."

"Splendid," he said. "Well, I'm sure she's okay. She's Hungarian. They're complicated but completely amazing women." He smiled at Babette.

"Yep. It's just weird."

"Join us for a drink?" It was a little after noon.

I sighed. "I've got to get some work done," I said.

"Some angels need to be freed from their stone?" he quipped.

It took me a second to understand him. Then I stupidly said, "I've been writing. Since she left, I've just kind of been alone. Not talking gives you so much space to think. I'm working on a novel."

"Oh," he replied, smiling. "I didn't know that about you."

"I don't really talk about it."

"We certainly don't want to disrupt the next Great American Novel."

"Yeah," I said, irritated.

"Just kidding, old friend. How about later? Up for some merry-making? All artists must live. There's a Zima release party tonight. The Hungarians have finally made it into the twentieth century."

"The drink?"

"Malt beverage! Some PR firm is throwing a shindig. Free booze. Waitresses in Zima-themed attire."

{five}

THE PR FIRM was only able to get one case of Zima so everyone at the Paris-Texas was drinking Guinness and champagne. Ellie and Margaret were there in one of the few booths when we walked in. Ellie wore a shoulder-length blond wig and smoked from a long golden cigarette holder with rhinestones encrusted around the barrel. I stopped at their table.

"You got in just in time," Ellie said.

I looked around. It was early. There was even room at the bar. "It seems pretty dead?"

"No, I mean Budapest."

"'Got in'?"

"I can almost remember the moment. In Picasso Point last weekend. Hundreds of new faces. Wide-eyed Americans, goatees and notebooks. The word is out. The party is over. At one time it was possible to know every American in Budapest. Now there are thousands of us. And I feel like it just happened this June. Your arrival seemed like the trickle that started the flood. I guess we go home now."

"Do you want me to get your coat?" This was the conversation that wouldn't die. *It* had been going on for four or five years. When *it* started and when *it* ended. And who was legitimately part of *it*. It was becoming clear there never really was an *it*.

Across the room, Marsh and Babette were standing at the bar, surrounded by three or four Americans.

Ellie watched me watching them. "Is everything okay?"

"I'm fine."

"You look like you've lost weight."

"I'm fine."

"Have you found work? How's your girlfriend? Gisela? She was nice."

"She wasn't my girlfriend."

"Oh."

"But, yeah, everything is fine. I don't know. You want a drink?" I pointed to the bar.

She shook her head, but kept looking into my eyes.

I started walking away. "That coat comment?" she said.

I turned. "Yeah?"

"It wasn't funny, Anthony. It was nasty. I don't think Marsh is a good influence."

As I walked over to them, I was blushing again from the dream. When I arrived at their circle, Marsh was telling the Americans he was going to buy a castle. Throughout the Hungarian and Czechoslovakian countryside, there were old castles that had been annexed by the government during Communism, but now with the free market moving along, the government was unloading them. You could buy a thirty-five-room three-hundred-year-old castle with a moat for forty thousand U.S. dollars. He said some of them even came with the original serfs who were now in their nineties and had been hanging around the castles for the past fifty years like orchestra members deserted by their conductor.

He segued into a rant about monarchy being the best form of government. "England hasn't had civil war in over three hundred years, solely because of our glorious monarchy. The Sex Pistols, arguably the most revolutionary thing to happen in England in the past fifty years, are a perfect example of why monarchy is a superior form of government.

"Having dissident citizens sing stupid catchy songs about the heads of government, instead of actually killing them like your people did to the Kennedys, or to start nationalist insurgencies within the government and general population as they are doing in Yugoslavia, is much healthier. When you have a clearly defined leader who is put in power by something as absurd as blood, then your opposition will always look too foolish to ever actually succeed in overthrowing some old lady in a crown. Plus none of that messy voting and campaigning. The millions of dollars that get put into campaigns can get put to real use, like arming occupational forces in Northern Ireland.

"As far as I can tell, democracy is a result of a society unable to produce a ruling class. It is an impotent culture. Men are equal in the fact that they are all losers, lacking in ideas and taste, unable to create a ruling class."

"Dude, we kicked England's ass," some guy pointed out.

"Dude," he said mockingly. "England dropped you like the plague. All historians agree that if we wanted to hold on to America, we could have. With minimal effort. George put up a slight show just so the French thought we had troops over there, but in truth we wanted to get rid of that mosquito-riddled shithole as much as the colonists wanted their so-called freedom, so that they could continue with the quaint little institution called slavery."

"Just be thankful you're not speaking German right now."

"Thanks, G.I. Joe. Thanks for all your help while they were bombing London to smithereens." He paused and took a drag from his cigarette. "Speaking German right now? If I was speaking German, you'd be speaking Japanese, fool."

Then Marsh turned from them and began as if they weren't there: "American males are such senseless wankers," he said to me. "Don't you think?"

"Someone should kick your ass," I said.

"Ah, Anthony, *malus americanus,*" he said. Then he turned to Babette. "Shhh . . . they can sense when you're talking about them," he said.

"I would have bitten your cheek off."

"Ah, his violent outburst, the biting and tantrums, et cetera . . . It's just fascinating."

He saw I wasn't laughing. He took a step back and clasped his hands. "Just having a bit of fun," he said. Going all Merchant Ivory on me. "Having a go. Nothing personal. Glad you could make it." He held out his hand.

Who isn't a sucker for the British? Their accents make you feel like you're in a movie. They are of an antiquated system. You are young and bounding into the future. You own the future. They can have the dusty old past. You let them be wittier, better read, more worldly, in the condescending way you let your grandparents tell you about savings and the virtues of a "good job." Because ultimately the world belongs to Americans and no matter what the British do, what they say, what they read, they will always be slightly less than you. This isn't true with all foreign countries, just the British. They're close enough to compare.

We continued drinking. I kept thinking about the inside-out dick. What he would do if I told him. Even if he were gay, this would probably freak him out a little. But the drinks were making it so I wanted something to happen, and history told me that's how you find your friends: you drop something messy on them.

Even if I wanted to, I wouldn't have been able to get him to stop talking. He had a connection or story for everything. He was an ass, but his mind was encyclopedic. Despite never having been near the area, he knew where my hometown, Skaneateles, New York, was. "Between Auburn and Syracuse. Up in that area where the towns are all named by the Greeks and Romans: Utica, Troy, Rome." For all his exact references, his American stories were openly and spiritedly clichéd. He had been offered a blow job in Greenwich Village. He had a friend from Kentucky who drank whiskey and shot guns. The London musical industry survived almost solely on the tour groups of fat middle-aged Midwesterners. But there was some mystery to the American that he was missing. It was easy to recognize the clichés about Americans, but not so easy to see why we were the world's lone superpower. And why that superpower seemed to be controlled by average white guys not unlike myself.

There were other people at the bar, but it was like the day on the veranda. When he said something funny, he looked at me to see whether I laughed. He bought us a few rounds of drinks. I was a little shy and nervous about talking. His mind was intimidating. But when he started poking fun at an American girl who seemed to be picking up an English accent as she drank, I jumped in as well. Then we were suddenly buddies, teammates on Club Alcohol. I began to think that this was what he liked about me: my frat-boyness, my beery averageness. And this was okay. It was slightly insulting, but I felt I could prove him wrong. My lack of education and thick-headedness could be turned into a stoic quiet confidence. I'd play the tough, silent American and he the know-it-all dandy. Hemingway and Joyce joking and brawling their way through Paris.

When Babette had had enough of being ignored and abruptly announced she had to go, he pulled me outside with them. Beyond the dark buildings, there was still a sliver of blue being pancaked between night and the western horizon. The sun was setting later and later. He kissed her unabashedly as I stood there like an idiot. We put her in a cab. He said he'd see her later in the week. He shut the door. He turned to me: "I'm going to marry her."

"She's nice," I said, but I didn't get their relationship. It didn't make sense that they were getting married. And to be joking about marriage, a huge mystery to me, seemed jaded in an unsettling way.

"Off to the Cracked Joke!" he said.

Every full moon, the organizers would squat at a different deserted building. At the beginning of each month, only a few people would know the location, but as the days progressed, more and more were let in on the address, and by the end of the month, these deserted buildings would transform into the best clubs in town. Then they packed up and moved again.

The city was cooling from its first day in the eighties. A warm breeze shifted through the streets, created by hot air escaping from the pavement. The air smelt yeasty with spring pollen. It all made me think of sleeping for the first time with nothing but sheets.

From outside, the building looked bombed. Scabs of gray plaster peeled from its sides. Every window was boarded over or smashed in, like dark eyes. Marsh guided us around to an alley where a bouncer stood at a hole in a wall. A red carpet led inside, but rusty rebar poked from the cement. Wires ran along the ground and lights hung from exposed pipes.

The bouncer asked us for that month's joke.

"How do you get a dog to stop humping your leg?" Marsh said.

The man nodded, waiting.

"You suck its dick," Marsh said.

The bouncer smiled then motioned us forward. We ducked our heads and stepped in. We followed a dimly lit path through cement debris and curls of chicken wire. After fifty feet, there was another door and a woman in a ball gown nodded and turned. We followed her. She led us through a dark hall with bare walls, which covered you with a white dust if you brushed up against them, and then down a set of stairs into the basement, a honeycomb of rooms, each cell with a different feel. A rave. A junkie's den with luxurious red couches, and people lying around shooting up or dry humping. A complete replica of an English pub. A bondage room, floor to ceiling covered in rubber. A poker table. After a once-through, we headed to the pub and sat down at the long bar and ordered beers and espressos.

By now I was drunk and I wanted to impress him. I told him about Gisela disappearing and her confession and in more detail how I'd really gotten to Budapest. Despite his intellect, he had the ability to put you at ease and make you think that whatever you were saying was serious and interesting. A combination of genius and naivete. After I finished, he asked, "But what does this say about you?"

"What do you mean?"

"What sort of person are you that you would just up and leave your life? I mean you had a job, a nice flat. You lived in the posh City of Love. What does that say about you, or about Americans, that they can just drop everything and bugger off? That is an unattainable luxury to most of the world."

"Well, we've got it pretty good. Is that really news?"

"Do you think you're common to all Americans?"

"As in 'average'?"

"Yeah, do most Americans not care about a job or their futures? You seem pretty content just being an aimless hang-about. Is that an American aspiration?"

"I'm not aimless. Stuff just happens. It's random that I'm here. I don't know. I had a job."

"A job you didn't like, a job you didn't know why you were doing. You said you didn't even know what you were doing."

"I kind of knew what I was doing."

"I can't tell if Americans are like our upper or lower class." He pulled from his Gauloise and watched the red ember burn while he held and then exhaled the smoke. "I mean, in many ways it is very aristocratic to just blow off everything, to be a man of leisure, but at the same time in Great Britain upper classes are generally far better educated than you, so they can pass the time doing fairly laborious and rewarding things like translating something or other. Or amassing a Faberge Egg collection. Something that would take some homework. Not what you're doing. Just kind of being alive. Just floating about."

He didn't seem to be saying this with any malice. I was his subject and he was free to pontificate.

"Do you follow baseball?" he asked.

"I hate baseball."

"Football? American football?"

"I'm not really into sports."

"I thought Americans loved baseball. The national pastime, and all that."

"And England's is watching her empire crumble?"

He feigned hurt and then sipped from his beer.

"Americans used to have it down to an art form, but it seems for today's Americans the most common form of rebellion is to become completely mediocre. Lease a Neon, get a belly ring, buy some wicker furniture from the Pottery Barn. What do you think?"

I smiled but didn't answer. Behind us, across the room, I noticed a woman who looked like Gisela. She was sitting in a booth with a man who was speaking to her intensely. They had been there when we came in, but in trying to be indifferent to the world I hadn't looked at them closely. I distractedly turned from Marsh, who was starting to give me a headache. I stared, wanting her to look back.

"What would you do if you could do anything?" Marsh, still talking.

Her hair was up and she wore a cream blouse and, I could see under the table, faded Levi's. She looked un-Hungarian.

"I could teach you things, you know. Oxford is a serious institution."

She looked into my eyes for a second. I smiled. She looked away, and pushed her ice cubes around with a straw, nodding as the man continued to speak. Why would you approach a complete stranger who sort of looked like someone you'd slept with? Why would you approach any woman who was so out of your league she was probably in an entirely different sport? Why would you approach a strange woman with a strange but clearly well-put-together man?

"What do you think?"

He and I had been drinking for over eight hours now. But Gisela was in trouble. She had to be. She and I had made love. She thought I was a nice guy. All I had to do was show her my rawness. She'd see how skinny I'd become. What did a freaky British guy know about the point of life?

I put my cigarette out and stood up. The crowd had thinned and now the room seemed brighter than when we had arrived. Drunk couples were the only ones left. The men were scrambling to say that one magic unknowable thing which gets her thinking it's okay to go home with him.

The woman resembling Gisela ignored me. The man looked at me askance. I pretended he wasn't there. I waited for her acknowledgment. She lifted her eyebrows and looked up out of the corners of her eyes, squinting, like peering up at the sun.

"*Jo este,*" I said.

"Yes," the woman answered.

"Gisela?"

"I'm sorry?"

"How are you?"

"Fine, thank you."

"I've been thinking about you."

"Do I know you?" She looked to her friend.

"What's going on?" I asked.

"I'm sorry, I don't think we know each other."

"Can I buy you two a drink?"

She lifted her glass demonstrating her drink. I held out my hand and told the man my name. He didn't say anything. He squinted at me. I turned back to her and gave her a "who's the asswipe" look.

"We're fine, thanks," she said. "Could you please excuse us?"

"I think about you a lot."

"I think you have me mistaken."

"I'm not a good guy. There's more to me. I'm difficult. I've been starving. I haven't eaten a square meal in four days." She lifted her eyebrows again and exhaled loudly, then turned away to the wall.

The man stood. "Go," he said. "Go away." His English was limited.

"No."

Is it me, or does everyone seem to know martial arts these days? I went down immediately. I sat on the ground for a second trying to figure out what happened.

"Go," he said again.

I stood up and pretended I was done, wiping my pants off, then swung at him kind of side-armed. I was immediately down again. He stood there waiting. My balls had been squeezed into one. I put my head between my knees. She stood from the booth, stepping over me. I looked up. He pulled some money out and flicked it onto the table, carelessly, as if it was something he couldn't get rid of fast enough, then said something to the woman and they left.

"What did you just do?" Marsh asked when I limped back to the bar.

"She's my reason," I said.

"That chap's arm candy?"

"I thought it was Gisela."

"What did he do to you? Your eye is turning a kind of guacamole color."

"We've slept together. I don't know why she left. It's fucked up. We weren't fighting."

"Anthony, your eye looks very off."

"I feel okay. Maybe just need some air."

"'Maybe just need' a doctor."

"I don't. I need her."

"That wasn't Gisela. She didn't look anything like her."

"She had the same hair and eyes. The exact same hair."

He had ordered us another round. When the bartender returned with the drinks, he stared at me for a minute, then walked away. The punch had momentarily sobered me. I asked Marsh for a cigarette.

"I've seen her," he said after a sip from his new beer.

"Who?"

"It was harmless. But I was with her last week. We went to Pécs. I'm doing a story down there."

"Gisela?"

"Yeah," he said. "But nothing happened. She just called me asking about the refugee camp and I was heading down right when she called. I invited her, assuming you were going too."

All the drinks kind of landed on me at once. I felt lucid and clever, then I couldn't walk. The room swam. I pulled strongly on the cigarette, and my throat immediately constricted. Barf tickled my inner ears.

"Okay," I slurred. "Okay, I have to go."

"It was nothing, my friend. We just took the train down together. I barely even saw her."

As we walked home, we weren't talking. I kept stopping to puke. Dawn was rising around us. The city not fully awake. Pigeons clucking and taking flight as we'd start down an alley. I couldn't stop spitting. Then for the first time in my life I heard a live rooster crow—then Marsh said, Watch this, and cockadoodledoo-ed. Seconds later a rooster answered him. Then another. People kept them in their courtyards, and, to this day, roosters crowing at dawn in the metropolis is one of my fondest memories of Budapest. Then he asked me if I was a good driver. He said it like it was a skill. Like typing.

"I'm okay. Why?"

"I might need one."

"You don't drive?"

"Gentlemen don't drive," he said.

We stopped at the Nyugati Station. My apartment was directly across the river and he was going north along Ot Utca. His eyebrows furrowed as we said goodnight; he was considering me in some way, thinking about my or all Americans' pointlessness or maybe how I was taking the news about him and Gisela.

"Marsh, my life is fine. You can have her. I don't care," I said.

"Yeah, I know. Don't worry about it, chap."

"There's no problem here." I could hear myself slurring. "I don't think I was being clear in there. Most of us don't float through life. We have plans. We have direction. Lots of direction. I've got direction. I'm writing a novel." The few sober brain cells begging me to shut up.

"Ah, yes . . . The Novel."

"Well yeah, kind of a novel."

"Kind of a novel?"

"More a collection of short stories with the same characters."

"Story collection?"

"Kind of an in-between."

"An in-between story collection and novel?"

"Yeah."

"Sounds fascinating."

"It's good. It is."

He looked at me and smirked. "Anthony, go home."

"I have direction. I do. I have tons of direction."

"Anthony, go home. I know you have direction. I don't think you don't have direction. That's not what's on my mind."

"It's about eighty percent written. It needs some work but it's not bad."

"Anthony, I don't care."

"Do you want to read it?"

"I'll buy it when it comes out."

"You don't believe me." I wanted to touch him.

"Anthony, it doesn't matter. You'll be fine. Look at your shoes." I had hundred-and-fifty-dollar Kenneth Coles on. "You're a prince. You'll do something interesting." A prince! "Listen, I've got to get some sleep. I'll talk to you later. Have a good night."

"It's both in the first and third person. It kind of switches around."

"You're going to need these." He handed me two pills. "Good night." As he walked away, his eyes on the ground, he pulled the belt of his leather jacket tightly around him. I headed inside.

I took the pills. I started a cigarette in bed as the rising sun began to heat up the room. I opened my notebook and reread the last thing I had written. I crossed out a few words then put it down. Light creeping across the uneven ceiling. A prince. My hand holding the cigarette on my chest, rising, then slowly falling.

❖ ❖ ❖

Hungover, but grateful for having thrown up, my skin squeaked against the porcelain as I lowered into the large kitchen bathtub. I pulled the thin curtain closed though the apartment was empty. I was jittery. I could see out of it, but my right eye was green. I was going to have to go home. The only two people I knew, my only two friends, were sleeping together behind my back. I'd call my parents and plead for plane fare. Go to New York and hit my uncle up for a job at MetLife. As soon as I'd bathed and eaten something. The water slowly rose around me. Despite everything else being emaciated, my belly puddled at my midsection. I wondered whether Hungarians jog. My flaccid cock floated in a seaweed of hair. I began to softly tug, telling myself to calm down. Just burn one out and then deal.

I envisioned my Top Ten Sexual Experiences collage and quickly hardened after focusing on an afternoon I'd had in my high school girlfriend's parents' bedroom. She'd let me stand while she lay back on the bed and put her feet on my shoulders and let me move in below and her ass was rubbing against the top of my thighs and my memory was letting me almost feel the weight of her feet on my shoulders and I began to speed up. The water lapped lightly against the sides of the tub. I pressed my feet against its base. And a tremendous orgasm was coming on, like baseballs in a batting cage machine, lining up at the bottom of my scrotum, getting ready to launch through me.

Keys clicked and the apartment door opened about four feet from the tub. The violent motion of yanking my arm away made a telltale splash. She stood there for a second and then walked over. She slowly peered around the curtain.

"It will fall off if you do that too much," she said.

"What are you doing here?"

"In Hungarian it is called *Nemi önkielégítést végez,*" she laughed. "It means to 'not be nice to yourself.' Make sure you drink a lot of fluids."

The water suddenly felt cool and greasy. My dick stupidly sticking up out of it. The huge canyon of difference between getting off and getting caught. I hugged my knees and I asked where the hell she'd been.

She pulled the curtain back. She paused, taking it all in. She smiled pityingly, more or less wincing. I was still hard, but with my knees up, it had sunk into my groin making it look like a hairy little mushroom down there. An extra roll of flab seemed to have bubbled out of my gut.

"To see more children," she said, lifting her eyebrows and cocking her head slightly.

"With Marsh?"

She paused. "Not with him. But he helped me," she said.

"Why didn't you tell me? That is such a bullshit move."

She let the curtain fall back. Her outline stayed for a second, then dissolved. She sighed. "You need to change that tone of voice," she said.

"You left without telling me. What the fuck."

"I didn't want to get you involved. That woman was serious about the police. You said so yourself you couldn't get arrested."

"What would have been wrong with telling me?"

"You would have been cool with me going out to Debrecen and Pécs without you?"

"Cooler than sitting here having no idea where you went."

She came over and pulled back the curtain again. "You sound stressed out."

"I'm going home. I've got to get out of Budapest."

"You need a vacation from your vacation?"

{ six }

Asher's door was closed when I walked in one night. I could hear a girl in there with him. They were both laughing. Her voice was slurred by drink and muffled coming from behind his door. But I had no reason to suspect it was Claire.

Then the woman was shrieking. Feigning attack. Saying "Don't, don't, get off me," until she made a little whoa and there was a pause and then there was the sound of her hitting the floor and then she was laughing. Like she fell from Asher's bed. She thumped softly. It didn't sound like it hurt. It sounded like she fell with drunken disregard for the wooden floor that she landed on. Asher said, "Whoopsy daisy" and started cracking up.

"My name's not Daisy, jerk," she said.

"Hey! Watch the language, cunt."

Asher Lavery gets laid. He's a completely different species than me. His universe has thousands more women who love to have sex in it than mine does. He's handsome and fun in a completely asshole-ish way. He also has that Fucking-Me-Is-a-Great-Idea glow. So the rough love going on in his bedroom didn't really faze me.

People who know us ask me why we are friends. I don't really have an answer other than: you should have seen him when he was young. He was an exciting teenager to be around. Most of us were pimpled, graceless losers in dumb clothes, stuck in Central New York, playing lacrosse, occasionally wrecking a parent's car, but he was that kid in high school who got the French teacher to buy you and your friends cases of O.V. Splits, got her to take you and him skiing in Vermont over Martin Luther King weekend. And, for about three weeks after his graduation, got her to leave her marriage and move into a condo with him. (There was a blunt and anticlimatic end to their romance; Mr. Lavery drove over and parked in front of her house for hours, refusing to leave until Asher got in the car with him. She moved to North Carolina.) But still, all of it, in Skaneateles, New York, was in a league of its own. It was like Asher Lavery had gone to the Olympics or something. Just lived a different life than us. I tried to get him to talk about it and he just said, "She was a crazy chick, man. She was fucked up." Our French teacher, the crazy chick. And although when we were roommates in San Francisco and he was heading south pretty quickly, he was still riding on that raw ability, that fucked-up charm. The ability to say, "Okay, this is life right now. Let's make it happen. I don't care about tomorrow. Let's just be huge, this very minute." Even if he used that ability wrongly, even if he ends up lonely and disease-riddled, I will always see him as a glowing, raging seventeen-year-old. My friend who has sex with French teachers. Someone who could do what the rest of us couldn't, who could make any moment a glowing golden thing. I appreciated him for letting me be friends with him back then, and it seemed wrong to ignore him now that we were older and heavier and supposed to be serious people. So we were roommates and, for lack of any real competition, he was my best friend.

There were no messages on the machine. I thought of calling Claire. We had had a small fight the night before: I was drunk, up on some moral

pedestal, bitching about how San Francisco is a hypocritical racist city because it pretends to be so liberal but keeps all its blacks over in Oakland.
I also thought San Francisco was humorless. I thought we should move
to Nova Scotia, somewhere real. Claire had said my anger was about
something else and I was a coward for not addressing the truth. I had put
a cigarette out in her Cosmopolitan and stormed off.

I took my coat off, hung it on a hook, and tiptoed past the phone and
Asher's door.

I went into the dark kitchen. I moved my hand along the cool, al-
most damp, wall for the switch. I found it and flipped the light on.
Everything looked surprisingly good. There were no dishes in the sink.
Cabinets were closed. A half-empty handle of vodka sat on the table.
Someone had wiped down the counters. I entertained the thought I was
in the wrong apartment.

I went for the fridge. I remembered Charlie Rose was interview-
ing Bono. Three Rolling Rocks sat where I'd left them. I snagged one,
uncapped it, and, after realizing the show didn't start for another fifteen
minutes, sat down at the table.

Asher walked out of his room. He was naked. His cock was hanging there, still a little stretched out from sex, wearing a light blue condom. His cheeks were flushed and his lips, red and full. This is how
he looks after basketball, I thought. And the size of his schlong? Other
guys' cocks always look bigger, but his really is huge. It's about the size
of a baby's arm. And he loved it. He stood in the doorway, stuck his hips
out, and wiggled it a little. The condom, dripping off the end, like blue
snot. It looked like Gonzo's nose. He walked over and grabbed a beer
from the fridge.

"Hey," he said.

"Hey," I said.

"What are you doing here?" he asked.

"Pretty sure I live here."

"But why are you home? I thought you were going out with those dudes at work?"

"Yeah, I bagged."

"Where's Claire?" he asked.

"Not sure," I said.

"You think she's home?" he asked.

"Could be," I said.

"You guys broke up."

"What do you care?"

"I just want to make sure. I want to know where you're at. I worry about you, man."

"Yeah, we're broken up. I hope I never see her again."

"Okay, okay. Chill out, Rambo. I was just checking." He drained another slug from his beer and then scratched himself.

"Will you put something on?" I asked.

He sat down. He picked up the sports page from the table and draped it over his groin. He crossed his legs, holding the paper in place.

"You have a cigarette?" he asked, reaching across the table toward me.

I pulled two out and we started smoking. I was reading the part of the paper that he wasn't wearing. He just sat there smoking and, I imagined, getting cold. After I finished an article about O.J., I looked up and asked who was in his room.

He looked at me for a second, then smirked. "Claire," he said.

"Claire?"

"Claire Murphy."

"My Claire Murphy?"

"Uhm . . . I don't think I'd call her 'yours.' Unless you're cool with me fucking her," he said.

"What?"

"You want me to repeat it."

"Seriously?" I asked him, looking in his eyes.

"Seriously," he said. "She came over tonight, kind of drunk, looking for you and you weren't here and we started talking and the handle of vodka was out and then ka-boom, the thigh-slapping commenced. But as you'll notice, I wore a condom. So don't sweat it."

"This is not happening."

"She said you guys were broken up."

"We've been going out for more than four years."

"That's present-passive."

"Dude, shut the fuck up. She's my girlfriend."

"My friend, she *was* your girlfriend."

His door opened and Claire walked out into the hall. She was naked too. Claire is no Gisela, but she has a phenomenal body, especially her ass. We had talked about marriage and the one thing I kept coming back to was her ass. It outshined all the other very good things about Claire: her good heart, her artsy, well-paying job, her tidy nice family back in Princeton, her mother who seemed to like me, her Volvo. There had been days when her ass cured my hangover. It looked as good naked as it did in a miniskirt or a pair of Levi's. Her ass made you think you could live off doggy-style alone. But standing there in the hall her ass looked a little tired, and the rest of her body pale and rubbery. Her garish red lips amplified her paleness. She had definitely reapplied her lipstick before coming out.

She saw me and tried to cover herself. One hand over her crotch and the other banded across her boobs. But then, and I can't imagine what the thought was, she decided to let her hands drop back to her sides, and she started laughing. An oh-look-who's-here. The combination of confidence with being buck-naked was disarming. There was a sinking feeling in my stomach. Maybe this was the norm for my Claire? In her other life.

Drunk Party Girl of the Universe. Weird sex. Oils. Plastics. Texas. Guys with mustaches. I'd been playing the cuckold for years. But then her laughing turned into hiccups. And she lifted her right arm in order to use the wall to steady herself.

"Hi, Claire," Asher said. "How you doing, baby?"

She straightened and shook her head at him. She continued down the hall toward us.

"Mr. Nova Scotia." She pointed at me. "You were supposed to be here."

"This isn't happening," I said to Asher. "This is not happening."

"Hey, Claire, you want some more vodka?" he asked her. "You want a little drink-drink?" Holding up the bottle and wiggling it back and forth like a sock in front of a cat.

"Mr. Nanook of the North." She started toward me. My hands rose from my sides. But she seemed to lose her train of thought when some spittle on her lower lip caught her attention. She wiped it off, smearing her new lipstick across her forearm. Then she looked at me again. Her face was breaking, her eyes starting to well. She started to say something, but then just seemed exasperated. She made a slight breathy moan. Then looked me directly in the eyes. She mouthed, what looked like, "I'm sorry." Then she hiccupped. Then she closed her eyes.

Asher looked at me, grinning. "She's a doll, man," he said.

"Claire, are you okay?" I asked.

She stumbled forward into the bright lights of the kitchen.

"You were supposed to be here," she said again, but this time more mad than sorry.

"Claire," I said softly. "Claire, come on, put some clothes on." I turned to Asher. "Stop being a dick."

"You," and she moved forward, pointing at me. Then in a sharp fast motion, her foot shot out. She had stepped in water I had tracked in.

She went horizontal, then down hard. The apartment shook. Bottles on top of the refrigerator clinked. We all sat there for a second, waiting for things to settle, to see if she was hurt. Then she moved. Her butt squeaked on the linoleum. She started to crack up. "You are an asshole," she said, looking up at me. "The hole of an ass. An asshole." Her left leg was bent awkwardly underneath her. She looked like a broken manne-quin, but also really clean under the bright light. I felt a rush of pride that she wasn't turning me on.

"This is pleasant," I said to Asher.

"Hi, Claire poo. Hey, baby," he said.

"Asher, get her out of here."

"Hey, I bet she'd sleep with both of us. Huh, Claire, want to double your pleasure?"

"Asher, shut the fuck up. And stop this."

"What?" he asked. "What's your problem?"

He stood. The newspaper clung to the sticky condom. He crum-bled and balled it up around his crotch, pulling off the prophylactic as he did so. A string of semen slopped onto the floor. He walked over to the kitchen sink. He opened the cabinet beneath it. He tossed the sports-page-slash-condom in the wastepaper basket and pulled a brown paper grocery bag out of the stack of them. He snapped the bag open and put his arm into it and smoothed the crinkles. He walked across the kitchen and put the bag over her head. She took a second to react— but was soon shaking, like a dog trying to dry off. I don't know why she didn't try to use her hands, but after another second, she exhausted herself and lay down backwards, which looked like it was going to be fine until, at the last millisecond, her head kind of sped up and smacked the ground solidly. You could hear her head kind of bounce in there. She went quiet.

"Voilà," he said. "No more Claire."

"Take it off." But I couldn't help myself and I laughed a little through my nose. I guess I snickered.

"Fuck that, dude," he said. "Isn't this the girl who just fucked your best friend? Fuck her. You shouldn't have to look at her."

"Asher, take the bag off her head."

"First let me get a picture. If she wakes up and has any ideas, we can send it to her mom. Or her boss."

Pictures of anything that you do after 9:00 PM are generally a bad idea, but I had never done something like this before and I guess I felt it was probably not the kind of thing that would occur regularly in my life, so why not? I could already see that I would someday, when I had outgrown this, whatever this was, confess the experience with heartfelt regret. Maybe to my wife? And this confession would bring us to a new level of closeness, and she would feel comfortable confessing her own sordid secrets, like the winter semester she LUG-ed out with her college roommate. Just something I didn't know about her, which would add another dimension to her already multidimensional, interesting personality. Not a thing to define her, but a thing that made her even more interesting. And she would feel the same way about me telling her the story of the time my roommate and I put a bag over the head of my naked passed-out girlfriend. These stories would bring us closer, make us more interesting to each other.

Asher had stolen about a dozen disposable cameras from a wedding he had attended a few weeks before.

"Smile, honey. Let's see those pearly whites! Pretend you don't have a bag over your head."

I don't know why. I know it wasn't the right reaction. It didn't seem funny. But we were both laughing pretty hard. Not really at Claire. If anything, we were laughing at ourselves. It's not like we felt we were being mean. We had been to expensive colleges. I had a subscription to

Harper's. We were just cracking up at everything. Him naked, a camera, our close friend passed out, a woman we had shared; it felt giggly, like an X-rated Benny Hill.

I'd done bad things—as teenagers my friend and I broke into the home of the Feinfelds, the only Jews in our town, every Saturday morning for years while they were at synagogue an hour away in Syracuse and raided their liquor cabinet and stole Mrs. Feinfeld's Valium—but this didn't feel like that. This felt light and jokey. If Claire hadn't been knocked out, she would be laughing along with us.

"She looks pretty well-done on that side. Maybe we should flip her," he said.

He grabbed a spatula with his free hand and held it out like a sword, trying to shimmy it under her incredible ass. Pretending she was a burger and he was going to flip her.

"Hey, take a picture of us at the barbecue." He handed me the camera. And it felt like Asher was beginning to leave me. I know that's what they all say. *It was all just a joke and then Dave slammed the car door on her by mistake.* But really, he suddenly was just off. Dancing around with his big dick. Poking her with the spatula. "This one is going in the yearbook," he said.

So I snapped some pictures. A few regular, then some landscapes. All the while, a little voice in the back of my head said, "Don't get them both in the picture." But then something strangled the owner of that little voice and I heard myself ask, "How is her mom going to know that it is Claire, if she has the bag over her head?"

"Always thinking, aren't you?"

He leaned down and carefully tugged the bag off her head. She looked okay. She just looked like she was in a deep sleep. Tuckered out. I snapped a few shots.

"How do you like your meat?"

I pretended to think about it for a second. Then I said, "Medium-well."

"Any condiments?"

"Nothing special. Salt. Pepper. Some ketchup, but no mustard."

He grabbed both shakers from the top of the fridge and began to salt her. Then he loosened the top of the pepper shaker and dumped the whole thing on her stomach.

"Oh, fuck, who did that? Who's the comedian? Who loosened the top of the peppershaker?" He was howling. Just gone.

Her eyes opened. She looked directly at me. I stopped laughing. She looked wide-awake. Sober, even. Her eyes did not seem mad, just disappointed. They seemed to say, "Don't you have a mother? I will someday be someone's mother. What if this had been done to your mother?" But as she was going to speak, her eyes closed again.

"Asher, stop," I said. He hadn't seemed to notice her waking.

"I haven't gotten to the ketchup yet. You want some ketchup, don't you? This dried-up burger needs some ketchup."

"Asher, don't."

The ketchup was stuck. He was slamming it with the palm of his hand.

"Slow and easy." Then it started to glub-glub out of the bottle onto her belly. He moved up and down the length of her body, slowing for each breast and her downy crotch. She stirred, not opening her eyes, but her body tensed from the cold ketchup and she rolled over onto her stomach. Her terrific ass like a target, like the change basket at the toll-booth on the Golden Gate Bridge. He poured some on that.

"She wants to get spanked."

"I'm out of here," I said. "This is fucking horrible. The kind of thing that ruins people." Although I felt myself smirk again.

"Hasn't she made a go at ruining you?"

"Man, not like this."

I stepped over her and walked back down the hall and opened the front door.

"Dude, come back."

❊ ❊ ❊

Once out on the street, I moped around the Mission for a few hours, feeling blown-apart and filthy. The air was humid but cooling from the green fog that sat like a ceiling just above the low rooftops. I bought a pack of cigarettes and walked over to the basketball courts on 19th Street and watched a midnight game for a while. Eventually I returned, half-expecting police, but everything was quiet. Asher's door was closed. There was still some pepper sprinkled around the floor like baby mouse droppings, but he had cleaned up the ketchup. I went into my room and lay in bed with my clothes on. Night passed slowly. I thought about going down to the police station and turning myself in. My eyes may have closed for an hour or so, but, in the clingy blue-gray morning light, I got up and dressed. I tried to be quiet as I snuck out, hoping that when they finally woke up, they wouldn't know I was gone, and they'd spend the whole morning whispering for no reason.

Claire called me at CNET at around ten and asked to meet for lunch. I was achy with sleeplessness. We went to Vesuvio's. She began by apologizing, but before our drinks arrived she was shaking her head and her neck was getting splotchy, and she was throwing "sexual assault" around. She was crying and we were only two blocks from my work. I didn't really do anything except agree and apologize.

If I have to point to a single thing that got me to Budapest, it was that night, weeks before I even met Gisela. I could never stand being in that apartment after that. It, and all of San Francisco, was covered with a kind of toxic residue. For the weeks that followed it felt like every woman I looked at knew. I felt my bone structure was changing. My eyes grew smaller and closer together. How do we let stuff like that into our lives? How do we live once it's there? I reexamined it over and over, and I could kind of blame Asher, but ultimately I had taken part in something completely mean and bad. I schemed on how to take it back, do it over, but ultimately you can't, can you? You can't take back the worst things. You can wake up and keep going.

{seven}

A SUMMER SHOWER BEGAN as we were pulling out of the station. The rain slowly darkened the buildings and washed the dust from the colorful Trabants. An hour later, the wheat and alfalfa fields of central Hungary shuddered under the still-falling rain. Then the weather cleared and from the west a low sun eked out under the clouds. Fresh swarms of blackbirds occasionally erupted from the trees as the train passed. She sat in the window seat and I pretended to be looking past her at the mustard-colored fields. Her skin was damp with perspiration. The henna coloring in her hair seemed to be fading and she was now almost her natural Japanese-black. The humidity in the air amplified her.

"Were you a Boy Scout?" she asked after over thirty minutes of silence.

"Boy Scout?" I shook my head.

"Do you know what the Young Pioneers are?"

"I can imagine."

"The Communist version of your Boy Scouts. Mostly interested in conforming, uniform wearing, and tying knots, useless skills in

general. Under the Soviets, every Hungarian child was one. We met after school and on Saturday mornings to sing Communist songs, practice
our Russian, and play these funny games that would prepare us for an
American invasion: Marching and How Far Can You Throw the Wooden
Grenade. We would charge each other with wooden bayonets."

She clutched an imaginary bayonet and made playful stabs.

"We were told over and over the horrors that awaited us when the
Americans came pouring in from Austria. Greedy, gluttonous U.S. soldiers would kill our parents and then eat us. The Americans lied to us
during the '56 Revolution, told us they were coming, to keep fighting a
battle we could never have won, when they never had any intention of
showing up—but we hated the Russians too. These fields here remind
me of those afternoons."

"You threw the wooden grenades?"

"Just little carved balls of wood with grooves in them. Whoever
threw the farthest won. I never did. Some of the boys liked it, but we
all knew it was silly. But who knows? Maybe they still do it. It kept us
busy and Hungarians have always had a special place in their hearts for
the absurd."

She was looking at me now and I felt we were connecting, getting
down past the oddness of even knowing each other, never mind sitting on a train together, traveling through the blowing alfalfa fields of
central Hungary to collect some orphans. She had tested me by taking
off and I passed.

"But even though I knew better, I didn't really like the idea of the
American soldiers coming. I was worried they'd find my dad. He had
left by then. My brothers and I were basically on our own, in and out of
institutions. And I was worried he and the Americans would get along.
They'd like him for leaving his bad Hungarian children. I wanted him to
be dead, but I was certain they'd make him a leader and I'd somehow be

punished or put in prison because he obviously hated me. Of course this was ridiculous, but it's how I felt."

The train was running along a marshy lake. She told me it was Lake Balaton. It was only twenty-five feet deep at its deepest spot, basically a flooded field. But at forty miles in length, it was the largest lake in Hungary. "The Hungarian navy keeps one of its ships there," she said. "The other one they keep on the Danube."

What she didn't tell me and I later learned from Marsh: Pécs is a border town, just north of Croatia. It's famous for its university. It's infamous for its proximity to the war. That summer, three years after Croatia had officially stopped fighting, the United States decided to step in and covertly back someone in the Balkan War. The HVO was trained and armed by the United States at the Taszár Air Base, a few miles from Pécs.

❋❋❋

Charlie, a Hungarian loosely affiliated with the Red Cross, who was apparently a contact of Marsh's, greeted us at the station. Gisela was hungry and he brought us to a café for a late lunch. He spoke American English and was tall for a Hungarian. His hair was white-blond, almost albino, like a short-haired Johnny Winter, and his head and hands were small. He moved in quick, avian movements, like his heart beat faster than most or he was in the beginning stages of Parkinson's. He had that kind of otherworldly devil-look albinos have and he never went for more than fifteen seconds without a cigarette in his mouth. He made me order the Cordon Bleu. The Hungarian version of this dish is paprika wrapped in cheese, wrapped in ham, wrapped in chicken and deep-fried in lard. He told me, "Take any dish, sprinkle it with paprika and deep-fry it in lard, and you will have the Hungarian version of that dish." He had our filled-out documents ready, but it was going to be a few more days before everything was in order.

After lunch, we took a cab over to friends of Gisela's, Lenya and Vic. Night was falling and a huge full moon was floating up into it. They lived in a small apartment building that sat alone below the overpass of a busy highway, isolated and apocalyptic compared to our place back in Budapest. The rest of the block contained empty, padlocked shops and an auto-body yard enclosed in rusty barbed wire. Gutted cars sat scattered behind the fence, prehistoric animals in the moonlight.

Lenya and Vic were friends from Gisela's own years in the orphanage. She told me they were adopted as stepbrother and stepsister, but they'd started messing around in high school and stayed together when they left the family. Now they were all the family either one had.

They looked as if they had just been dug out of someplace wet and dark. Their mouths were always slightly open, hinting at a constant bewilderment. Their skin was pale and slightly damp. They both had huge pupils. Vic wore his dark hair long and had a thin patchy beard. His body was small and compact with rounded shoulders, like a wrestler. But a light emanating from his large green-gray eyes bumped him up into an entirely different attractiveness bracket. And Lenya, the same. A plain woman with bland features. An oval cheekless face. Weak chin. Hair severely parted down the middle, the color of dishwater as a result of over-dying. But then glowing gray eyes that seemed to catch all and any light in the room and throw it back at you.

They were some kind of orphan-archetype, like if you looked under "orphan" in the encyclopedia, there'd be a picture of Lenya and Vic. They were disconnected from a past, but also shame or guilt. I was conscious of being the only non-orphan and kept wondering what that meant. I felt guilty for having had, pretty much, an incredible childhood and having been absolutely ungrateful for it. These people had survived with everything stacked against them. They were so much more than me. Everything I had started with my parents, started with love and food, with opportunity. But maybe that included guilt? I kept having the urge to take off my watch and give it to them.

Lenya and Vic didn't speak any English or German. None. My Hungarian vocabulary had swelled to and seemed to be peaking at three phrases: "Good day" *(Jo napot)*, "I don't speak Hungarian" *(Nem beszelec Magyaral)*, and "I would like a large glass of beer, please" *(Egy nagy korso sor, korsenem saipen)*. Interacting with Lenya and Vic reminded me of being around the bobcat a kid in my dorm freshman year kept as a pet until it clawed the inside of his Saab—including the dashboard—to ribbons. You watched it more closely than a normal house pet, and it always seemed to be watching you.

They had made us steamed peas and roasted potatoes. We felt bad that we had already eaten. But not too bad—they seemed to think a cereal-sized bowl of peas and plate of fried potatoes was a proper dinner for four people. After they finished eating, Vic broke out some homemade *palinka*. He and Gisela spoke casually while Lenya cleaned up. I watched whoever was talking, pretending to follow along. When the dishes were done, we moved into the cluttered dark living room. I sat down on the couch. Vic quickly motioned for me to stand back up. I did, thinking I might have sat on something fragile. He kneeled next to me and reached into a hole in the upholstery hanging from the bottom of the couch. Using his middle and forefinger like clamps he pulled out a bag of white powder. I looked over at Gisela. She had been watching me watch Vic.

"Coke?" I asked her, impressed.

She shook her head.

"Speed?"

Again she smiled and shook her head.

I had never shot heroin. After reading Burroughs in high school it was something I always felt I should do. And having read *Jesus's Son* a half-dozen times in the previous two weeks, the moment seemed almost fated. But when I actually saw the crinkled, yellow-white baggie, I wasn't so sure.

Vic stood and went into the bathroom. He returned with a rolled-up piece of red felt cloth bound by a white pipe cleaner. He undid the pipe cleaner. The cloth unraveled. A small plastic bottle slightly bigger than an eyedropper, a tablespoon, a rubber hose, and a syringe spilled onto the coffee table.

He poured some into the spoon and wet it with a few drops of water from the bottle. He slowly moved the low flame of his Harley Davidson Zippo under the spoon. The ingredients started to sizzle. A small white cloud of smoke poofed out. The heroin dissolved into a tea-colored liquid. He sucked it into the needle, and offered it to me. I shook my head and nodded to the women. He insisted. I shook my head again. He looked at Lenya. She already had her shirtsleeve up. Her arm wasn't riddled with holes like in every junkie movie; the inside of her elbow was smooth and alabaster. Two thin blue lines snaked down her arm about a half-inch apart. Vic chose the outside and, I thought, slightly smaller vein. Holding her arm steady with one hand he tried to pop it in, like a Sunkist, with the other. It wasn't working. He stopped and held the needle to her skin and slowly pressed. She squirmed. He held her arm tight, and then, in a blink, the needle was in her. A second passed while he tried to see if he got the vein. A smile came to his lips and he emptied the syringe into her arm. Her eyes closed. He slowly pulled the needle from her. She bit her lower lip. She started to sway a little like she might pass out. Vic had her by the shoulder. She took a deep breath. He let her lie back into the couch. He wiped the needle with the red cloth and motioned for me.

"Are we sharing the needle?" I looked at Gisela.

"It's fine. It's just a little dull," she said.

"I'm not using that."

"This isn't America, Anthony. There's no AIDS."

I shook my head.

"Anthony, they get dull. It's not a problem."

Vic tugged at my shirtsleeve. I clamped down on it with my other hand.

"I'm not doing this," I said.

She translated for him. He looked at me and then at the floor.

Then he smiled. He began nodding. He said something in an enthusiastic tone to Gisela. She laughed and replied, of which I understood the word *Nem*. But he was adamant. He looked at me and opened his mouth wide like someone trying to show his cavities.

"He wants you to drink it," she told me.

"Drink what?"

"Just open your mouth."

He demonstrated by opening his mouth and lowering the needle in. I opened my mouth. He came at me, lowering it in as if he were going to skewer my tonsils. His thumb moved. The liquid hit the back of my throat. It shot up into my ears. Some dripped into my nasal cavity. The taste, like aspirin, clung to the sides of my throat. I suppressed a gag. Vic put the needle down. I smiled and waited to feel something. He shook his head a few times, then lifted himself from the couch and went into the kitchen. He came back with a small mirror, poured some of the powder out, and sliced a few lines. He handed the mirror to Gisela. She inhaled half of one and gave it back to him. He took the other half and then another whole. Then he went through the business with the spoon again and shot up.

A silky warmth began rising through me as I watched him. Consciousness flickered. I thought I heard someone say I'd won something, but didn't hear what. Then the warmth began to fade and I felt the liquid in the back of my throat and was suddenly slightly nauseated. It was like I was coming down with a sore throat or there was water in my ears. I told myself to chill out; it was just a drug.

Lenya and Gisela each snorted a line and after watching with motherly satisfaction as I did one, they disappeared into the bathroom. Vic and I began a short volley of the mirror, but he seemed content after shooting up and offered most of the lines to me.

Heroin is the opposite of coke. Instead of feeling amped and witty and ready to fuck models, you feel warm and full of love, primarily for yourself, but definitely with enough left over for others, until the possibility of heroin running out surfaces. I was wondering about them in the bathroom and wondering whether I would fool around with Lenya if the opportunity were presented. I decided I would. After each line, Vic smiled at me, and me back at him and it was slowly understood that this drug was the best thing ever, that people who did heroin were members of an exclusive and brilliant club who had sex with each other's girlfriends if needed.

The women eventually came back out. They weren't dressed different. They hadn't applied makeup. I was proud of myself for thinking this was okay. The evening began to slide by, and Lenya and Vic became without a doubt the coolest people I had ever met. We still sat on opposite sides of a huge canyon of verbal communication, but they were clearly feeling as great as I did and so I just knew they had to be the coolest. I wouldn't have been able to fool around more than a hug, and the idea of swapping girlfriends now seemed from a more sober cynical moment that my fifth line had cured me of. Now, not before, everything was really perfect, we were prefect, the most content I'd ever been in my life. The dirty dull needle seemed like a funny little soul-exposing thing that only enhanced the evening, something I could chalk up to experience, write about. Gisela was so peaceful for a gorgeous person. I kept telling her she had the skin of a princess.

Near midnight Lenya and Vic floated into their bedroom, and Gisela and I took some cushions from the couch and put them on the living room floor.

Our clothes were off. Our skin taut and electric against each other. Ends of her hair tingly and warm on my stomach when she knelt over me. Like being swiped here and there with moleskin. Her mouth was on and off it. Inside I felt as if small cups of warm water were exploding throughout my body, starting at my feet and moving up and then back to my feet, running through me in waves. I nudged her off and moved on top, suckling, kissing her breasts and shoulders and pressing my groin into hers. I moved lower and lower trying to get there. But she steered me away when I got too close and finally I let it go on her stomach.

In the morning, over black bread toast and espresso, Vic handed out Valium, like vitamins, to deal with our achy parched hangovers. Drugs are the only universal language.

The orphanage was directly adjacent to a refugee center, a dusty collection of tents where the main activity seemed to be playing basketball. Gisela told me the building that now housed the orphanage had at one time been a pillow factory. It was a blue cement structure with faded green lettering printed across the wings of an equally faded goose that soared through some shabby clouds. Inside the building there were no factory parts, but two rows of bunk beds and one long metal picnic table. Outside, a few basketball nets had been erected on pads of dirt and dozens of chaotic worn paths snaked through surrounding fields. They didn't seem to go anywhere. They were tracks of anxiety. The camp's inhabitants walked them constantly, in groups of twos and threes, discussing what must have been a bleak or completely unknowable future.

I read later in a Red Cross booklet that the war had displaced over four hundred thousand people, the majority of them Bosnian Muslims. But the kids at this place seemed gypsy, and a disproportionate number of them were missing limbs or psychologically damaged, or "Special Needs," as Gisela called them.

Hungary took in fifty-five thousand refugees before closing its Croatian border in 1992, mostly women and children, and more of the latter than the former as parents sent their kids, hoping to spare them the fighting. But then the parents weren't spared and were killed. Three years later the majority of the refugees were still in Hungary. And an unholy number of them were orphans. You'd think this would make Hungary a good place to find children. National disaster, man-made or natural, creates parentless children. But Gisela explained that for them to be legally adopted in the United States, the INS needed the parents' death certificates and proof of no living relatives. Acquiring these is nearly impossible in countries full of death camps.

The work-around to the adoption process was to sponsor a child on a six-month humanitarian visa. Once the child was in the United States, as long as they weren't asking for a job or welfare, they weren't a problem. Some palms would be greased and the child absorbed into the normal adoption process. She told me it was done all the time.

Thin dirty kids were paraded in front of us and we were invited to eat with them. Most of them knew a little English. They weren't super-curious about us. They kept asking how long we were staying—like they were trying to gauge how much effort they should put in—but they didn't have the eager look in their eyes the St. Eszter's children did. They hadn't been orphans for all that long, or they weren't aware of their orphan status, and they still hoped to go home someday. Gisela told me we were only eating with them for their benefit, to entertain them: the children she was bringing back had already been selected. The holdup was a few compulsory background checks: just-for-show efforts to find out whether the parents were really dead; and Form I-600 (which said Gisela and I were a sane couple from the Bay Area with a nice home and good income from my job as a product manager at Cisco), which was supposedly cross-checked.

The Valium from the morning was receding and I was beginning to feel hungover and nauseated. A sweet young kid, Alexi, followed me out when I went for some air. He wanted me to play tetherball with him. He was four feet tall. I'd barely touch it and the ball would whip around out of his reach, gaining speed as it wrapped the pole. He seemed sincerely wanting to win, but when I let him, he'd shake his head, pissed that I wasn't really trying. I eventually refused to play anymore. He pleaded. I continued to refuse. Then he begged me to take his picture with the clunky 35-millimeter I had had since college. I took one. He almost peed himself with joy. He begged for some more. I faked the rest so I wouldn't waste film. He showed me his muscles. He did a half-assed cartwheel. He pinched his cheeks, pulling his eyes down and top lip up. A female worker, bottle-feeding a small baby, had started watching us. After a while, she came over and offered to take a picture of both of us. We exchanged the bundled-up baby for the camera. I couldn't believe how light it was, like holding a croissant that occasionally moved. In the picture, I'm cradling the baby and Alexi is leaning against me, looking up out the corner of his eye, smiling at me. When the woman was done and I had handed the baby back, she asked to see my passport one more time. She had forgotten, but she needed to make a photocopy. I didn't think twice and handed it over. She was gone for five minutes. She returned smiling. She told me I'd lost weight since the passport photo. She showed me her passport picture. She looked completely different: doughy, her hair was curly and in pigtails. In real life she had expensive-looking straight black hair with Egyptian bangs that showed off her large brown eyes. It made me think of Asher's quip about making sure to see a girl's mother before marrying her.

That night I made Gisela buy some chicken and rice and a bottle of Tokia and champagne for Lenya and Vic. Again we sat in the living room and after dinner relaxed with more heroin. Vic had gotten new needles during the day. He held up four blue packages, each was sealed and covered with German words. I had no defense now. After an anxious moment where he examined and then skewered my right arm, I was glad I didn't have one, because shooting up was so much better. The high was instant. A supreme and smothering calmness, an expansive commanding okay-ness. Everything felt perfect. The past, the future, nothing could be better. If someone was telling me I won something, I couldn't have cared less, because I had everything. Plus no itchy feeling deep in my ears. Addiction suddenly seemed like not only a real issue but also a slightly welcoming one. The world was fucked up because most people didn't do heroin. If everyone could feel this feeling, then it would be universally understood how good our species was capable of feeling. Why shouldn't everyone have access to this kind of beauty? We would benefit in the same way if everyone had fifteen minutes in front of Michelangelo's *David*. We'd have a world that would understand our potential for feeling amazing.

❖ ❖ ❖

The next morning at the refugee center Charlie slapped me in the head. It hurt. I backed away, looking at Gisela to save me from him. He kept raising his fist, shaking his head at me, speaking in a tight pissed-off whisper. It was kind of funny, because he had a cigarette in his mouth. He was so mad he couldn't speak English. But what the fuck? He took Gisela by her elbow and walked her away from the only permanent building at the refugee camp. A police car was parked out front. Only one car, but four guys dressed in tight blue pants, leather jackets, and knee-high motorcycle boots standing around. I followed Charlie and Gisela.

"You gave her your passport!" he finally turned and said to me when we were out of earshot of the police.

I suddenly realized Vic hadn't given us Valium that morning. It was as if beetles were under my skin, my heart had been replaced with a bag of ice, and someone was standing next to me clapping in my ear. "No heroin" was a disease if the disease Tundra Leukemia exists. I couldn't believe I had only done it twice. I vowed either to never do it again, or never stop doing it.

"Did you?" he was asking me.

"Did I what?"

"You people are doing something highly illegal, and you think it's okay to show your passport."

"It's my fault," Gisela sighed. She took her hands to her eyes and rubbed. She didn't seem to be feeling as bad as I did. I wondered if Vic had given her Valium on the side.

"It's over," he said. "They know he's not who we said he is."

"Does she want money?" she asked.

"No, I'm done with this. You need to go somewhere else. This is my job. I'm sorry."

"What about my money?" she asked.

"I'll get it back," he said. "But I need a few days."

We got back in the same cab that brought us.

I had given someone my passport and apparently I wasn't supposed to. How was this a problem? Why are there no Hungarian jokes? Because the country's too inconsequential. People with no power take the trivial and banal and make it matter. Gisela didn't believe Charlie.

She thought he was making this up after she'd given him four hundred dollars for his help. There was no way the woman would care. Gisela was pissed.

We drove back into town and had a beer and coffee. Then we went to a matinee: the dubbed Michael Douglas movie *Falling Down*. Gisela just needed to think.

When we came out and our eyes adjusted to the light, a large cloud was inching forward, letting some sun lance through the street, illuminating dust and creating small pockets of warmth.

"I need to make a phone call," she said.

"Are we going back to Budapest?"

"This isn't over. Charlie has my money."

We continued for another two blocks and then found a small restaurant, walked to a table in the back, and sat down. She ordered us two bowls of goulash.

I was confused. Deeply mistrustful. Thousands of miles from home. Slightly addicted to a narcotic I'd never be able to get in my real life. I looked at the cause of all these things and wanted her to do something, anything, with my dick, hold it, blow on it, pet it, put it inside her, something.

While we waited in awkward silence for our goulash to cool, she left for a minute to make the phone call. I let out a silent, gaseous fart, and began to breathe deeply as if I could suck in the stink before she got back.

"Your friend Marsh, the funny guy, is stopping on his way to Croatia. He's going to help us with Charlie," she said when she slipped back into the booth. "I'm not interested in your opinion on this."

❄ ❄ ❄

The rail tracks were laid in dusty rust-red stones. The wire fence between the two sets of tracks also was covered in this unhealthy-looking red. An old woman sat hunched over on her luggage clipping her toenails. Small black sparrows darted in and out of the station house, which seemed to be stuck in a state of mid-renovation. The train was metallic-gray with green lettering. Marsh hugged me when he got off and gave Gisela a double-cheek kiss. We had gotten high again the night before and while I was high, it seemed hilarious that Marsh was coming down to help us. But now that he was here and my jones-ing was starting, it seemed dangerously stupid to depend on him for anything. Marsh was smart, and maybe he had boned my beautiful Hungarian girlfriend, but he didn't seem a reverser of fortunes.

"I've got two hours until the afternoon train. I need to be in Trieste tonight, to catch a ride to Rijeka," he said. I almost hit him in the face.

As we took a cab to the refugee center, Marsh said that Charlie bailing didn't seem like the Charlie he knew. Gisela explained I had given my passport to one of the do-gooders, who realized the name of the husband on the forms and my name weren't the same and started asking questions. People here from international organizations got involved because of the refugee status of most of the children.

"What do they care?" Marsh asked.

"They shouldn't. They're just feel-good democracy creeps spending other people's money," she said. "The heavy hand of 'helping.'" She laughed. "He stole my four hundred dollars."

We pulled up. Marsh and Gisela got out of the cab and went into the main office. I waited in the cab. A few minutes passed. Marsh came out and lit a cigarette. Another couple of minutes passed. Gisela walked out with the woman who had photocopied my passport. The woman looked bemused, nodding her head in understanding, but not agreeing to anything.

Gisela and Marsh walked back across the lot. Gisela opened the back door and slid across the seat, dropping her hand on my knee. Marsh got in up front. Charlie was in town and wouldn't be back until later in the afternoon.

As we drove back into town Marsh looked up into the rearview mirror and said, "You guys should come with me."

"He has my four hundred dollars."

"All of these people were in Rijeka before they made it here. There are thousands of people, literally dying to get out. It's just five hours south."

"I think we should go back to Budapest," I said. "If we can't convince Hungarians, and Gisela's Hungarian, I doubt we're going to have any luck in another country."

She was watching the road. "Croatia is Hungary three years ago. Marsh is right," she finally said.

"There were thousands of people fleeing Hungary three years ago?" I said. "There was a war in Hungary with mass graves?"

"No, Anthony," Marsh said. If he kept using my name, I was definitely going to hit him. "Rijeka isn't dangerous. I've lived there. It's on the sea. It's beautiful and safe. Just a mess, the infrastructure. But there are thousands of children who need help and who aren't caught in this bureaucracy."

Her hand was again on my leg.

"We can rent a car," he said. "I'll expense it."

"You don't drive."

"You do," he said and smiled.

She softly scratched the top of my thigh with her index finger. "It'll be fun," she said.

"What about your money?"

"I got ripped off. Wouldn't be the first time."

Marsh was looking straight ahead, smiling. Then he turned and looked back at us both. I held his look, and he looked away and his smile straightened.

{eight}

As we walked down the smooth worn sandstone staircase that wrapped around the interior of Vic and Lenya's building, the air was cold and still, but up beyond the roof clouds blew in and out of sight. People had put their houseplants outside their doors to bathe under the day's sunlight and now their vines hung from the railings, casting little spills of darkness across the walkway. Lenya and Vic leaned over the railing, watching us as we went, yelling things to Gisela. Vic had inexplicably begun crying when we told them we were going. Then he packed us onion and lard sandwiches for the trip. We pushed open the heavy wooden doors and walked past two cats rustling around in the garbage.

The sky was blanched pink and blue as the last light of the day faded. Street lamps were beginning to light up. Small wafts of air, created by day turning to night, pushed through the streets.

As we walked to the rental car, a Trabant, Marsh lectured us on the Brontës: what they wrote and did. I hadn't realized there was more than one.

At the Trabant, he sat down on the hood and pulled out a cigarette while I wrestled our bags into the tiny trunk. It was still light out, but his cigarette ember was more distinct than his form, making me think of the Cheshire Cat. Gisela stood next to me as I moved the bags around, examining her hands.

"We can get wine outside the city, but if we want anything hard, we should get it here," Marsh said when I finally got the trunk shut.

"If I'm driving, I think I'll be okay if we just stick with wine," I said.

Gisela looked up and asked if we could take a picture before we did anything. I took my camera out. Marsh pulled a camera from his tote bag that had a flash almost as big as the body.

She found an old babushka-wearing woman waddling down the *korut* with a burlap bag full of potatoes. The lady was confused at first by the size of the camera, but once she realized which button to push, she excitedly snapped our picture as we stood under the glow of the street lamp.

As she handed back the camera, she was laughing and saying *"Szép, szép lány,"* telling us over and over that Gisela was a very pretty girl, a lovely girl. Gisela blushed and mustered up a polite laugh but in fact she looked less lovely than I'd ever seen her. The heroin had caught up with her and now she looked how I had felt earlier in the day. Her face kind of damp, glazed in sadness, her eyes barely open and her lips were almost purple.

We thanked the old lady and began piling into the Trabant. Marsh, maintaining that driving was undignified, climbed into the back so he could lounge about. He sat sideways with his feet up on the opposite window. Gisela and I got in up front.

"Are we sure?" I asked her as we were pulling out.

"Yeah, yeah. Just get me out of this fucking city." She was staring back up into Lenya and Vic's window. Although they had done nothing but assist us, her look carried disgust.

It took about thirty minutes to get out of Pécs, but once we were on the main highway, headed south, Gisela pushed the cork into the wine bottle with her apartment keys and we started drinking. I hadn't driven since Claire and I had rented a car and driven to Carmel for a weekend months before. And although the night outside was black, I could sense the expansive countryside. I pictured long fields of corn, rows of grapevines and string beans. Wooded knolls. Herds of roadside trees crowded into the headlight, and when they fell away it was as if they were marching off the edge of Earth.

It felt good to drive a car. A straightforward physical task. There were so few things you could just do as an expatriate. You couldn't, for example, mow a lawn. You couldn't clean your gutters. I crouched over and pushed and pulled on the stick shift in quick rapid jolts. I held the tiny steering wheel tightly. The car handled like a golf cart.

Eventually we stopped for gas. Marsh wanted to fill up before crossing into Croatia where he said everything was in spotty supply. He also wanted Vic's onion and lard sandwiches out of the car because they stank. In the station, we bought more wine and some chocolate, and then back outside, in the parking lot, some Russian prostitutes hit me up for a cigarette and then laughed at the Trabant. Marsh's mom was White Russian and he loved to speak the language. He taunted them, "It's the only type of car your loser pimp boyfriends won't steal." To most Europeans, vodka, prostitutes, and car thieves seemed to be Russia's only exports.

This upset the prostitutes. They started screaming at us. They looked Gisela up and down. They gave us all the fist-to-the-crook-of-the-elbow. There was a volley of Hungarian between one of the women and Gisela for a few seconds. We got back in the car.

On the road, everyone was quiet, and as I drove the little car with its dim headlights, the outside world seemed huge—so much bigger than anything I could wrap my mind around, immense to the point that it didn't seem to exist at all. In the silence, I'd watch the headlights creep along the bushes and fields. And most of the time it was like the night outside of any car anywhere—we could be on our way home from a basketball game at the Syracuse Carrier Dome in the middle of January—but then our lights would cut onto a horse-drawn cart or a stumbling drunk man with no shoes being walked home by a little boy, and I'd feel invading and superior.

Marsh told us that at the Hungarian–Croatian border the customs officials give you cool stamps. Gisela said they were stickers, not stamps. White stickers with a red and gray coat of arms and a little crown. They take up a whole page in your passport.

We arrived at the border around midnight. Trucks were running in neutral, lined up for about a half mile on the Hungarian side. Bugs rioted in the headlights. The war had been a big boost in Hungary's transition into a capitalist society. Border towns like Pécs flourished in the illegal arms and fuel trade with the Croatians. Even so, the border guards still made a big deal out of searching any kind of transport vehicle. We drove slowly past the trucks and sidled up to the inspection booth. Young men with guns came out and asked where we were going and why. Marsh did the talking. He showed them a press ID and had Gisela and me hand over our passports. They asked us to get out while they searched the car. Marsh and Gisela went to find a bathroom and I walked off away from the bright lights to stretch my legs and smoke.

Away from the street lamps, the sky became visible. There was no moon, but stars flushed the darkness, blaring and wild. I felt a cold dread. The last drop of heroin was inkling out of me. I started to tear up. I clinched my eyes and held my breath. To ground myself and calm down, I concentrated on the wire and tree shadows that sliced across the pavement at my feet. I was slightly drunk, my mouth dry, a small headache beginning towards the front of my skull. Those everything-is-nothing thoughts came. Everything is all a waste of time. The only thing in the world worth doing is being a doctor or a teacher. Actually fix people, make them better. I'm wasting time when there is so much shit to do. I breathe and eat, and produce nothing, just take up space. If I just had a little more H. . . .

The trees swam in the wind, but the only noise was the diesel hum from the line of trucks. The sound reminded me of an enormous refrigerator. I imagined them all shutting off at once, like when you walk into your kitchen at 3:00 AM for a glass of water and the room suddenly goes silent as if sensing you. I breathed again and turned back toward the car.

Marsh was telling Gisela that living in a country with a civil war going on next door made him feel at home. They had that in common. Of course I never wanted him dead, but I was definitely thinking about beating him up before the trip was over. As a kid, my grandfather told me the English starved to death eight million Irish. A guard pressed the cool stickers that took up a whole page into our passports, and we drove off.

❊ ❊ ❊

"This sounds corny," I said, "but I want you both to know that you influence me. I'm different because I know you."

They waited.

"And I don't know. I don't know what you two did but also don't care. I just want you to know you can always count on me for anything. If either of you ever need anything, even in like twenty years, just find me. If I have it or I can help, I will. I promise."

Still silent, waiting to see if I was joking.

"It's like, in theory, I just want to push us together into a little ball, almost a group hug, but not. I just want, for this trip, for our friendship to somehow mean something, something that will mean something years down the road. I want this to be a trip we remember. A thing we will call each other and reminisce about."

Marsh coughed.

"I'm serious," I said. "I mean . . ."

Gisela reached across the front seat and put her hand on my leg. The engine sounded far away. The wheel vibrated beneath my hands. She scratched at the top of my thigh with her pointer finger.

"Anthony, you're the best. You're a nit, but okay," Marsh said from the backseat. "Although shoot me if I ever need anything from you."

As he was saying this, police lights went on behind us. We were about fifty kilometers into Croatia. For a second I felt we were being arrested for my confession.

"What should I do?" I asked. Gisela's face went red, then black, then red. She was smiling.

"Just pull over. And don't say anything unless I ask you to. Don't show them any ID. Pretend you don't understand," Marsh whispered.

Through the rearview mirror I could see an army jeep. Military uniforms. Marsh rolled down his window. He spoke to them in a mixture of English, German, and Russian. I could follow the non-Russian parts. His big lie was that we were poor Hungarian students. They didn't seem to have a problem with this, but wanted me to pop the trunk. After a harried minute of searching futilely for the trunk button, I got out, walked around and opened it with the key. They kept asking Marsh if we were smuggling gasoline or guns or foreign currency. They went through our backpacks. They realized we weren't doing anything illegal, so they gave us a speeding ticket. They wanted approximately nine dollars and they wanted us to pay it now. We paid them with American dollars.

Before we left, I asked if I could take their picture. I held up the camera. Marsh rolled his eyes, but they gathered shoulder-to-shoulder with their guns standing at their feet. I was already imagining the moment when I'd gotten a girl into my apartment and as she was looking through junk I had nonchalantly sitting on my coffee table or maybe

I'd be using it as a book marker in my telephone book, she'd see this picture. On the back of it I'd write: *Croatian Infantry, Croatian Border 2:00 AM July 1995.* The girl would read it. This would lead to story after story of the time I spent in a war zone and until she couldn't stand it anymore and had to have sex with me over and over and since I had been to a war zone I was all too aware of our mortality so I would make love like it was the last thing I would ever do in my life and it would go on and on until dawn.

One of the men thought a Hungarian student taking his picture was funny and fired two shots into the air. Then they laughed and talked among themselves, and finally, as if an afterthought, they waved us on.

"They were saying that only poor Hungarian students would drive such a piece of shit," Marsh said. "It seems they believed us."

Soon Gisela and Marsh fell asleep, and as they slept, I joked with myself that it would be funny to drive off a cliff or onto a wrong road towards Banja Luka, a place I'd heard about on television, where it was pretty probable one of us would get shot, or at least hurt in ways we never could have imagined before leaving home. How brave it was for me to be driving through the night in a war zone. I said, ha ha. I sat up straight and barreled my skinny chest out as if to be the epitome of brave. I made some machine-gun noises. Ra-ta-ta-taa, ra-ta-ta-taa! Young Anthony and trusty companions travel through the night, I mouthed into the silence.

I eventually calmed down and checked the map. A tollbooth was coming up outside Zagreb and we hadn't changed any money yet. Still worried about driving at night, I decided we should remain poor Hungarian students for the rest of the ride so we wouldn't have to show anyone else our American dollars.

Gisela woke up as I was telling the tollbooth guy in clunky German that I would like four tomatoes. He leaned out the brightly lit booth, like he was going to grab the car. He explained forcefully, in English, German, and Croat-Serbian, that Hungarian money is no good. When he paused, songs from a small radio trickled out from behind him.

"No, no, no! Not good!" He chucked the worthless money I had given him back into the car.

He wanted about sixty cents. I just started making noises.

"Cowalaca, Amos *und* Andy, iceberg, carphone. *Verstanden Sie?*"

"Carphones? *Nein! Nein verstande,*" he said. "I *wollte deutches, american-ish oder croatianish Geld? Verstanden?*"

"Wir sind armen ungarish Studenten. Wir haben keine Geld."

Marsh woke. It took him a second but he told me the man didn't want our Hungarian money. I stopped, waiting to see if the tollbooth guy heard this. The man began to rage. He put both his hands to his eyes and slowly dragged them down his face and gray beard. He threw his hands up in the air. He pointed into the car. In English, "You think I'm a fool? You are trying to steal from me. If you do not give me the money, then I have to pay. I pay for you to drive in my country. *Verstand!?*"

"Danke." I wrestled the car into gear.

"No! No!" he screamed as he scrambled from the booth, out into the path of the Trabant.

At first, as he was running alongside us, holding onto the door handle, there was an immediate thing to react to, like having a fish on the line or dinner burning in the oven; I drove slow enough so that he could hold on.

"Anthony, Anthony! Stop. He's got the car. Stop."

The man looked into my eyes and I felt deliciously full of verve. Just doing something, making the moment happen. Wishing Asher was here to witness. It seemed like forever, but once I floored it and the man fell away and I could see him on his ass through my rearview mirror, my verve turned to fear.

"What the fuck?" Marsh demanded.

"He'll be fine. I can see him getting up." I continued to strain into the mirror. The guy was still down, watching us drive away, his left hand holding his right elbow.

Gisela stared, her mouth open. She was going to sleep with or distance herself from me real soon.

For a minute no one said anything as I drove.

Then Gisela: "Whoa."

"Really, Anthony, what the fuck was that about?" said Marsh.

"I'm the driver."

"You're the asshole who is going to get us killed."

"I didn't want to show him our dollars. You're the one who wanted us to pretend to be Hungarian."

"He wanted sixty cents."

"Yeah, but if he knew we had dollars he would have wanted more. And he would have telephoned up ahead to some of his friends, and told them we were coming. Anything goes," I said. "Now calm down. Stiff upper lip and all that."

"You're completely fucking mad! Like he won't phone ahead after he nearly gets run over. Gisela, do you believe this rubbish?"

"Anthony, the war is two hundred kilometers south. There is no violence up here," she said.

Oh, great, I thought, he has her now. I have a momentary loss of judgment, and Marsh gets the girl. This was so fucking typical. This is the way it always is. I lose the girl, because the pencil-dick I'm hanging out with pretends to be more levelheaded than me. Always, always, always. In high school, everything would be going along great. We'd be at a party. We'd be drinking beer. I'd be playing eye hockey with a relatively hot girl. I'd say something funny. I'd get on a roll. I'd start getting excited. Then I'd throw a bottle at a car or, as a joke, call someone's mom and tell her that her son was drunk and wouldn't give us the keys. Just something that would be slightly past fun, and the girl would stop talking to me.

I wanted to tell Gisela that Marsh slept with his fifteen-year-old sister's friends—which he did. Tear him down. What's that gonorrhea, I wanted to say. I have dreams about him, so he's probably gay. Do something, make fun of his accent, his pitiful country. My throat constricted. My stomach felt full and cold like I had drunk a gallon of gazpacho. My eyes moistened. But . . . I just stopped. It all turned off. Like I had suddenly leaped onto dry land. And I said, "You're right. I don't know what I was thinking. I just lost my head for a second. I really don't know what's gotten into me. I haven't slept. I haven't been eating well." And it felt like I had moved quickly through rough muddy thistled terrain. I swallowed and took a quick swipe at the tear in my right eye.

Admitting my faults, not fighting reason. This felt good even: to have done the bad zany thing, but to now be aware and apologetic for it. They were right. I've got to gain some weight. No one cares that three young foreigners were on the road. No one was going to rob us. But we were foreigners driving a 1973 Trabant. You can only legally drive them in three countries in the world. The third—other than Hungary and Yugoslavia—is Guam.

I looked at Gisela. She seemed to understand, or at least be faking sympathy for the entire car's welfare.

"Do you want to drive?" I asked her.

"You sure you're okay?"

"I just wasn't thinking. I think the speeding ticket shook me up. I'm really sorry." Marsh sat back against the seat and chuckled—something no American I know can do. And, I think, he began to envision how he would tell this story back at his drinking clubs in Soho.

We drove for another few hours in this fuzzy silence. Each of us scared, holding our breaths every time we saw another car. Then the

pinkish-blue sky began to get lighter than the land as we started up the
pass through the Gorski Kotar Mountains. The foothills were behind us.
The sun was rising, but we were in a pocket of darkness. As we drove
up through the pass, sunlight sheared across the hills, at first only catching the leaves of the taller trees like they were in spotlights. Then as we
slowly wound up the mountain road, the sun caught the rest of the forest,
yellowing everything, until eventually the world outside was brilliantly
green. Mist rose from the road and from small clearings in trees. Gisela
suggested we pull over and rest for a while. I was tired like you get after
a night of acid. My eyes ached, and I kept touching the back of my head
to test that it existed.

I pulled off onto a small gravel lot. Marsh said he was fine where he
was, still lounging about. I got my sleeping bag and walked off a ways
toward the woods, looking for a place that would still be shady when the
sun fully rose. Gisela was going through her green backpack.

I lay down and felt that sleep would be impossible. I bunched up my
face, pressing my eyelids tightly together. There was a damp dawn wind.
The grease of a night in a car covered my face and hair. I itched all over.
I could sense bad acne coming on by noon. It would be one of those
breakouts that make your face feel like it is going through your entire
adolescence in two hours. Then I was asleep.

❁ ❁ ❁

"Anthony?"

She was standing over me. I'd been asleep for less than ten minutes.

"Can I sleep over here?" she whispered.

"Of course."

She laid her sleeping bag down next to me and slipped in. I was very
awake again. My body felt waterlogged. My face heavy. The thin rolls of

skin on my neck were damp with sweat. But as she was getting comfortable, delicate small movements brushing against me as she shifted into place, the thin scratching sound of sleeping bag against sleeping bag, my groin stirred. I thought about the nights we had slept together. I pictured her below me. I pictured her naked walking around the apartment. Then she was crying.

"You okay?"

She didn't say anything. She pushed herself up against me. Her breath tingled on the back of my neck. The base of her stomach pressing on my butt, making me want to reverse our positions.

She sniffled. Where was she going to wipe her nose?

"What's wrong?" I asked.

"Nothing." Her arm went up over my shoulder. I shivered with thrill and wanted to put my lips on her wrist, which hung inches from my face.

"We should get some sleep," I said.

"My life is a mess," she said.

We were in the shade, but across the field the sun had hit and a haze of steam was rising off the tall dewy grass.

"Don't let me do any more drugs, okay?"

I turned around and faced her. "Dude, you're just hungover." I laughed. "You'll be fine."

She frowned and closed her eyes.

"Do you want to go home?" I asked.

"No. I've got to do this. I owe people so much money."

She hadn't moved when I turned around. Her face was inches from me. It hurt to keep her in focus. "How much?" I asked.

"If I get two non-special-needs kids, then seven thousand dollars per child, plus expenses, that would put me in good shape. This is the last time, but I need to make it happen."

"Jesus."

"Those people we saw, Mike and Lucy. They're probably paying twenty thousand per child. Just for the opportunity to come all the way over here and get dicked around. The people who will be taking the kids I deliver will probably pay twice. It's an ugly business. You can dress it up any way you want, but there are only two elements in this transaction: human beings and money. That woman who saw your passport was right not to trust anyone."

"Okay," I said, "let's just not worry about it. We're going to have a nice time. Try and not think about it. I've got some money in a 401(k). We can figure this out."

My head was beginning to ache from looking at her from so close. I rolled back, away, and she hung her arm over my shoulder again. Dew was slowly seeping through my bag. The birds had turned on. I drew my legs up closer to my body. But when I moved, she gripped me, pulling herself closer. I hugged her arm to my chest, hopefully signaling we had gotten somewhere. We had done this thing. But now let's just lie here in it and sleep. Nothing else was said and in the blue light of dawn I could see her hand and the gloss of her fingernails and I put my cheek against her wrist and eventually we slept.

{ PART TWO }

It Isn't a War Until a Brother Kills a Brother.

{ nine }

No one wanted to deal with the hotel or exchanging money, so we drove straight for the blue-green water, which had been in view since we cleared the Velebit Mountains. It was a little before midday. The sun burning and dense, but low on the southern horizon. The sky was empty of clouds, and there seemed no end to it, like if you stared up long enough planets would come into focus. We had the windows down as we drove through the narrow and cobblestoned streets of Rijeka. The houses were box-shaped and painted pastel greens, yellows, and pinks. They were built into and on top of one another, Venetian-style. The commercial and government buildings were faux marble and designed in a mix of Art Deco and Roman architecture. The Adriatic was ultramarine blue and, on that morning, flat as a millpond, bringing to mind David Hockney's pools. The shoreline, which we could see for miles to the north and south, looked like photographs I've seen of Greece, except the land beyond the rocky cliffs was covered in pine and the foothills leading up to the mountains were green.

After the city and then south for another three miles or so, I pulled off the road onto a small bluff that overlooked a narrow inlet. We opened the doors and fell from the car, as if stumbling from a burning building. The gravel crunching beneath our feet, we stood around, uncrinking our necks and scratching our scalps. It was so freaking beautiful.

"We should take a dip," Marsh said.

I said I didn't want to get all salty.

"Gisela? You care for a swim?"

"No suit."

"I promise not to look."

"You go ahead."

Slightly dejected, he shuffled down a thin dirt path toward the water. Gisela and I walked over to the railing and watched him until the path wound behind an outcropping of rock near the bottom and he disappeared from sight.

She pointed straight ahead, "Abruzzi." It was true Italy was on the other side of the sea, one hundred and twenty miles directly west.

After I took a picture of her, I let the camera drop and pointed about forty-five degrees to the right, toward the northwest. "Syracuse, New York." It was about four thousand miles from where we stood.

"There are a few things between here and Syracuse," she said.

"None that really matter. In my life."

She stepped in front of me. "Not one?"

Then Marsh yelled up from the water. "It's lovely. Get down here."

We walked closer to the edge. He was floating on his back about ten feet out from the rocks, his face buoyed in the slow waves. The rest of him was inches underneath the water and his blurred pale skin looked as white as an iceberg. Away from him, where there was nothing for the water to contrast against, the sea was the color of anti-freeze or Scope, and here and there, dark shadowy clumps wavered ominously on the sandy bottom. When he saw me aiming the camera, he sank beneath.

He surfaced further out and yelled up to us. His voice lost in the wind. Gisela mouthed like she was yelling, but made no sounds. He dove under and came up near the rocks directly below.

"No more seriousness," he yelled. "We are no longer serious characters." I felt this was a reference I should know, but didn't. Keeping it low so that he couldn't see, I brushed the back of my hand against Gisela's leg.

❖ ❖ ❖

After the swim, we drove back into town, and Marsh told us that before this latest war the Dalmatian coast had been Eastern Europe's French Riviera. This seemed right. There were miles of empty hotels and restaurants. The area had slid from tourist attraction to something soiled by the detritus of war in the past two years. Civic buildings and hotels had been turned into refugee camps. Smoked pigs' heads hung from the balconies of penthouse suites. When we stopped for directions or to let a woman with a cart full of melons cross in front of us, mobs of small children lurched at the car, trying to hawk jewelry made from bullet casings or pieces of rope and plastic. Not many other cars were on the road, but a few times we pulled up behind a farm tractor hauling a hay cart full of men. The thin brown men would cheer at us as we cautiously passed them going around the blind curves of the narrow windy road. They would whistle at Gisela and someone would yell "*Jo napot*" when they saw our Hungarian license plates.

We checked into the Hotel Meteor. The floor was marble. A large Venetian chandelier hung from the center of the lobby ceiling. On the walls there were paintings of various coats of arms. Two-dimensional lions with snakes for tongues. A knight with dragons perched on each shoulder. During its day—which couldn't have been too long ago—the hotel had been four-star, but now the elevator was out and Marsh said it hadn't been working since he first came here two years ago. There were no employees other than the young man behind the desk and he offered no assistance in getting our bags to the third floor.

As we trudged up the stairs, I asked Marsh why he didn't go to Sarajevo—a war city I had heard of.

He rolled his eyes. "Rijeka is the closest port city to the Krajin enclave," he said. "Five years ago Krajin was the site of the fiercest fighting. The local Serbs, with the help of Belgrade, declared it their own state. The Meteor, despite its crumbling grandeur, is the center for all illegal trade going in and out of here. Millions of dollars in highly illegal deals get made in the bar downstairs. Visas, guns, fake visas, fake guns. Thousands of people are trying to get out of this country. People just stuck in no-man's-land. And the borders to that no-man's-land are drawn up here."

"It sounds like *Casa Blanca,* but feels like an off-season Palm Beach."

"You know what, Anthony? You're kind of fucking daft. You think you know what war looks like?"

We were at the third floor landing. He looked at his key and then started down the hall. The maroon carpet had gold squares. The wallpaper was embroidered with gold vines.

"I just thought it would be different, I guess. Scarier," I said.

"You don't know what you're saying."

Gisela cut in: "Marsh, is there a pool?"

"No, there isn't a goddamn pool," he answered. "The ocean is right fucking there. The ocean is right there and there is a war going on just inland and you want a fucking pool?"

She laughed. "Marshy," she said, "calm down. Just a simple question. Just requires a simple answer. I understand you think you're

Bosnia Bob and everything, but chill out. What happened to no longer being 'serious' people?"

I thought he was going to cry. His forehead turned dark red like he'd been slapped. He dropped his bag and pulled his hand through his hair.

"Okay, okay," he said.

"Do Anthony and I need to find another place to stay?" she asked.

I wanted it so badly.

"No, of course not." He took a deep breath. "You're right. I'm sorry. I just didn't sleep. Both of you. Anthony, I'm sorry. I'm very glad that you both came. I'm really looking forward to this. I'm just tired and stressed. I have a lot to do. The Pécs story needs to be in London by Friday."

We stopped in front of a door. "You guys can have this room," he said.

"Why don't you two have it?" Gisela answered.

I looked at her but didn't say anything.

"I'm not feeling too great," she said.

"It doesn't matter to me either way," he said.

"Fine," I said.

The hotel was no longer serving dinner when we woke from our naps, but Marsh knew of a good pizzeria around the corner. Gisela wasn't hungry, so it was just he and I.

Both of us fat and dull with sleep. The pizza, its thin crust, was good but my tongue was thick. I swirled the chilly white wine around in my mouth, hoping it would clean my insides and wake me. We drank a couple carafes of the local wine during the meal and afterwards Marsh ordered a bottle of ouzo.

"D'Annunzio," he said, "armed a thousand Italian anarchists and vagrants after the war was over and took it upon himself to reclaim the former Roman Empire. He started with this city. He found homeless people in Rome and armed them."

"I thought the Italians lost the war?"

"No, they were on the winning side, but the Big Three treated them like dirt at the Treaty of Versailles. They had been promised all of the Dalmatians but got nothing. D'Annunzio said bollocks. And because the world was still reeling, and no one was about take a stand against another crazy anarchist, they just let him do what he wanted.

"He was racked with syphilis and deep in a cocaine binge the entire time. He was totally demented as he reigned the city," he said. "He gave speeches on the heroics of suicide. And every third Tuesday, he made the locals give up their redheaded daughters for the pleasures of the Empire. Girls were marched through the streets of Rijeka naked while crowds were forced on their knees to praise them. Then off to the palace!"

Behind Marsh, a fiery orange sun was sinking into the Adriatic.

"And he had nude statues of himself placed all over the city. Have you ever seen pictures of him? Some men should just stop with busts of their heads."

I had never even heard of D'Annunzio. "Who paid for all this?" I asked.

"The Plebs. He ruled the city for two whole years, from 1919 to 1921. Doesn't seem that long ago, does it?"

"Seventy-five years."

"Just seventy years ago redheads were publicly paraded through this city. A modern-day Babylon." he said. "D'Annunzio was onto something. Fun fascism."

The sky turned rose-colored after the sun was completely below the horizon, and thin clouds, like cotton candy being pulled apart, stretched towards us.

After, we walked back to the hotel. Gisela came down and we sat on the patio in the warm darkness and smoked and drank some more ouzo and then went to our rooms.

{ ten }

A SMALL BREAKFAST of espresso, rolls, and grapefruit juice. Marsh started making phone calls. I sat in bed, looking around. The curtains were filthy and stained with brown watermarks. The rug reeked of smoke. The walls were beige. But there was hot water. The bathroom fixtures were modern. The mattress had spring. The top blanket was about as disgusting as the curtains, but the sheets underneath were crisp and white. There was a feeling of things not being taken care of, but it was nicer than Hungary.

Gisela eventually came over. Marsh was still working but said she and I should check out the Hotel Splendid. It had been a beach resort but was now run by UNICEF and would be a good place for Gisela to start getting a feel for available orphans.

"Follow the shoreline," he said. "There's a path along the cliff going south. You'll come right up on it."

Out in the bay, hundreds of sailboats were moored. Two or three had their sails up and cut across the sea like water bugs. Further out, an aircraft carrier sat anchored on the horizon. When you looked away for a short while and then back, the massive ship jumped an inch to the right

or left, as if being flicked by a puppeteer's hand. I pulled my camera up
to take a picture. Through the lens the carrier looked toylike and lost its
context in the rest of the bay. I turned and pointed at Gisela. She had just
smoothed and let go of her purple light cotton dress. It was a summer
dress that stopped just above her knees. She was wearing white running
sneakers. She reminded me of Claire when we were in college. I loved
Claire in her short, thrift-store summer dresses, but for some reason, and
I can't remember what, she stopped wearing them shortly after we met.

In the picture Gisela's clasped hands are held against her stomach, stuck. She's not smiling and her expression seems to be saying,
"This picture is all about you."

We walked through town and then along the docks and waterfront
until we found a path that headed south above some low cliffs. As we
continued, the town noises began to disappear, and soon the only sounds
were the light gusts rattling the brush and scraping leafless branches
against the larger stones and the slapping of the waves below.

"I'm sorry about the tollbooth," I said.

"I had no idea how beautiful this was," she answered.

"I was just exhausted. And I guess I'm a little freaked out about
the war."

"It's okay," she finally said. "There isn't really a guidebook on this stuff."

"There should be. I'd buy it."

"But this isn't really the war. Everything we've read about for the
past three years has been south and inland."

"No, I know. Marsh's a little bit full of shit. This town doesn't even
seem to have policemen, never mind soldiers."

"Do you want to swim?" she asked. "I have my suit on underneath."

The sun was high now and the dampness in the air when we first got
on the path was gone. A swim would make showing up at the Splendid
seem natural.

"Yeah, totally."

Lizards chased lizards around the tree trunks. The light wind was tugging at her hair and dress. Her hair was wrapping around her face, into her mouth, until she cleared it with her hand, only to have it blown back again. We followed the path and began to hear classical music up ahead. We came up over a knoll and the path continued down to a beach where there were some people. Most of them were sitting on tables by volleyball poles that were being used to hang laundry. No one was sunbathing or swimming. And as we got closer, I noticed there were only one or two men.

The classical music came from speakers in the trees. Children engaged in a version of tag, their cries muted by the music and wind. Most of the women at the tables were smoking and watching the children. Some folded clothes. The building that had been the Splendid sat about a hundred yards up from the water. It was a large pink stucco structure with most of its windows boarded up. There was a fenced-off patio on the roof, which had a dilapidated cabana with an empty bar poking up from its center. A large piece of linoleum curled off the bar like a fingernail, catching the sun.

The women watched us as we crossed the beach. We kept close to the surf, trying to respect an unmarked perimeter around them. I smiled and timidly waved but no one waved back. In fact, although they were facing us, no one gave any impression of seeing us.

"Do you want to check it out?" I asked her.

"No, let's keep going. Maybe on the way back."

We were almost all the way across to where the path started again.

"You can't go any further," a voice said in English with a difficult-to-place European accent. We turned. A tall young man was jogging across the sand. As he got close, he slowed to a walk. He looked healthier than the other people. He was thin and shirtless. His Adidas shorts were too small, and blue with white piping down the sides. He had straight blond hair on top of his long face with cheeks so rosy the color almost looked like it was from exertion. He was more vivid than everyone else, as if he had eaten vegetables recently. The others were gray and sluggish, terminal patients who had finally decided to let it all hang out. The children stopped playing and watched him. He took long, but slightly duck-footed strides, leaving lonely pocks in the sand.

"Land mines," he said. "It's probably fine, but they haven't swept yet."

"Land mines?"

"Yeah," and he pointed up ahead of us, further down the beach. "But you're okay. Just don't walk past that fence."

"You're kidding," I said.

"Nope. But just don't go any further." Then he asked: "Are you British?"

"American," I said. "She's Hungarian."

"*Jo napot,*" he said to her. "First time in Croatia?"

"Yeah, we're on vacation," I replied.

"How do you like it so far?" He looked and nodded to Gisela, trying to include her.

"It's beautiful," she said. "There's something about the light and the air. There's a mist but it's sunny."

"The German Riviera," he said.

Just then the speakers went silent. We all looked up into the trees, then the music started again.

"Who are they?" Gisela asked, nodding in towards the women and children.

He offered his hand. "I'm sorry, I'm Thomas." Gisela and I each shook hands and introduced ourselves. He turned toward the building. "They're . . . we're guests of Women's World Health and UNICEF. I'm Dutch. I work for the latter."

Some of the children began to call to him. A small girl, whose legs seemed the same diameter from thigh to ankle, ran over and stopped ten feet away and put her hands behind her back and began to sway. She was wearing a grown man's undershirt like a dress. Red stains ran down the front. After Thomas still hadn't looked at her, she began stomping up and down. I lifted my camera and she threw her hands to her face.

"It *is* beautiful," he said. "You will like it. You should drive up the coast. Go to the churches, the restaurants. The Korkyra is very good. I love it. The risotto is better than in Italy. And the disco called La Conception. Tonight it is very good. Not every night is good. But tonight is. In Pula, there are Greek ruins. A coliseum. There's much to do."

"She's lovely," Gisela said pointing to the girl. "Hello," she waved to her. The girl kicked sand at us. Gisela walked over and held her hands out in fists, wanting the girl to pick one. The girl wouldn't and Gisela opened one hand to reveal a tube of cherry ChapStick. The girl snagged it and giggled. Other children headed over, and Gisela pulled back to us.

"They're so beautiful," she said.

"Some people don't think so," he answered.

"How not?. . .What's your name?" She called to the girl. The girl didn't understand and was busy showing the other children her ChapStick.

"La Conception is in town?" she asked Thomas, still watching the children.

"The edge of town. You can walk. Go west on the street called Adamiceva."

"Do you live here?"

"No, in town. Just a few workers live here. Most of us stay in town."

We said good-bye and that we'd hopefully see him later and then Gisela and I walked back along the same path. We hadn't swum. I wanted to push her down in the sand and just lie there.

"That is fucked up," I said.

"Did you notice there were no teenage boys? Fourteen-year-old boys. For once in my life, I desire to see teenage boys."

She paused and swallowed. She pulled the front of her dress up to swipe some sweat from under her chin, then left her hands in front of her face. Speaking through her fingers, "I'm not criticizing you, but Americans are so unbelievably lucky."

"Yeah." I wanted to have something intelligent to say. I wanted to point out reasons for or results of this luck. I wanted to see some connection between chance and democracy. But my mind seemed like a slushy river, congested with nothing, and the clearest feeling was the sadness that comes from not feeling anything when you feel you should. A bunch of war refugees sucks, but who was I?

I looked out on the water. I looked at the backs of my hands. I watched her shoulders, the cleft in her dress along her left shoulder blade. I looked closer at the prints on her dress. The factory outside Hong Kong where elderly women stood at the machines doing whatever weird and menial task it was that created and dyed that flower print. The factory next to that factory where blow-up dolls are made. I mean, yes, of course, it sucks that these people have to live in a decrepit beach resort with three hundred other people. Yes, it sucks that their husbands and sons were most likely dead in some mass grave in a nondescript ravine deep in a nondescript patch of forest in a nondescript piece of countryside. But how does it suck in my life? I have pictures of them that will eventually get me laid.

Gisela, a few feet ahead of me, seemed to be feeling something different than this. Her eyes were on the ground. Her shoulders bunched forward. Pressing one thumb into the palm of the other hand. She was probably having more practical thoughts than me, saving some children or herself. Drawing a line across the moral terrain of her life. Deciding which side of the line to stand on. Did she wonder about me, like I wondered about her? What I wanted from her? Was she as confused about me as I was about her? Don't you marry the people you can't figure out? Isn't that what you want in a wife, someone who'll always be a mystery? I took a picture of her back. Her hair lifting and falling in the wind. The dark blur of the aircraft carrier in the lower right corner. *My first wife feeling something.*

❀ ❀ ❀

Back in town we stopped at a café on the water. We both ordered a beer, Turkish coffee, and a Danish. I pulled out the *Lonely Planet* I'd snagged from Marsh. The sun was warm and tingling on my cheeks and neck. Down on the beach a mother dunked her baby in the slow surf. Old men crabbed from small cliffs that bordered the lagoon. They tossed animal scraps on strings into the water as they smoked cigars and talked and laughed loudly. No different than the Hungarians and their carp, except they were surrounded by sunshine and ultramarine water, and their catch, though bottom feeders, wasn't scarred dumb fish riddled with mercury. Sailboats flying German flags tacked across the bay.

Gisela closed her eyes and tilted her head back. She appeared to have suddenly passed out and was about to fall back in her chair, the front two legs of the chair leaving the ground, and as I was reaching for her, at the last second, she suddenly woke, catching herself. "You were going to save me? Anthony, that's sweet."

"What are we?" I asked.

"Me and you?"

"Yeah, are we together?"

"Right now?" She looked around. "Yes, we are."

"Are we sleeping together?"

"Not sure," she said. "We slept together in that field."

"Did you have sex with him?"

"Is that really any of your business?"

"I wouldn't be here if it wasn't for you."

A girl came out with our drinks.

"Why can't we just see?" she asked, sipping from her beer. Then she stopped and looked down at her glass. "Does this taste weird? Here, taste this." She held her beer up for me. I took a sip of mine. It was cold and better than any beer in Budapest.

"I don't want to share a room with him," I said.

"It doesn't taste rank?" she asked.

"It tastes fine," I said.

"Yeah, you're right, I probably can't taste anything anyway with all this medication I'm on."

A child carrying a chicken walked onto the patio and began to solicit customers to buy it. The bird seemed drugged. It sloshed in his arms. Gisela waved him over and reached out like she was going to grab the chicken. He squealed and jumped out of her reach. Then he bent over and stuck his butt towards us and took off laughing.

"What medication?"

"Just the usual." She picked up her purse and started going through it.

"Why are you being like this? What did I do to you?"

"Anthony, I've got lots of love. I adore you. You're a very very nice guy." She reached out and touched my arm. "I like what we can do to each other. But I have to deal. I owe people a lot of money. My plane ticket. The money that asshole stole from me. I'm on contract. I have to be thinking straight. Can't you just wait until we figure all this out?"

I opened *Lonely Planet*.

Our Lady of Trsat was built in 1453 on the grounds of an older church that had been built to commemorate the spot where some angels, who were carrying the house in which the Annunciation took place, had rested on their way to Rome. The locals wanted Rome to help legitimize the sacredness of the angels' resting area by giving the church another holy relic. In the fourteenth century Pope Gregory responded by donating a picture of Mary believed to have been painted by St. Luke.

"You want to check out this church? There's a painting by an Apostle."

"Less than anything in the world."

"What do you want to do?"

"Go back to the hotel and sleep for two weeks."

❖ ❖ ❖

I walked her back to the Meteor and got the car out of parking and drove towards Trsat Hill.

I parked in the empty lot below the two buildings and walked up a small path to the church. Inside the doorway an ancient woman stood to the side, almost enveloped in a heavy maroon curtain. She was wearing a blue frock that tied on the back and the front. She didn't ask for money and I didn't see any place to put any, but I held out some change from my pocket. She shooed me past. I pointed into the main chamber and she nodded, then looked away.

The temperature dropped and the light turned amber. The two-thousand-year-old painting sat on the altar. The Mother of God looked wooden and distracted. Her mouth was resigned and in a small grimace, but the longer I looked at her, the more she drew me in. Her right eye seemed to have slowly noticed me. Her forehead began to gain curvature and shape. The lack of detail now made her look stark, cold and alone, like a woman whose son had been sacrificed to a drunken mob for reasons she wanted to believe were good, but knew in her heart were just senseless and cruel.

How does a place where angels stop to rest eventually turn out half a million weary refugees in a year?

Sometimes when I'm alone, I have the sensation I'm being pulled up into the sky. Almost like I have a hook through my nose and I'm being reeled in. It doesn't hurt, and it's not scary. I just get up on my tippy-toes. My insides evaporate. My flesh becomes weightless fluttery stuff, the walls of a beehive. I don't hum, but my body kind of purrs, flickers, a long soft shimmer running though me. And I pull my arms close to my sides, my elbows under my ribs, and I put my chin up, facing the sky, like I'm trying to kiss a much taller person, basking in some big warm thing and everything inside me feels light and sparkly, and I'm supremely confident the world is good and that there's something bigger than us and that thing is good.

After these episodes, I often wonder if I'm schizophrenic.

I moved over into a pew and knelt, but after ten or fifteen seconds got up and sat and crossed my legs. Basically I know we're just atoms, stuff moving around, from leaf to bear's intestine to star to Thomas Jefferson's hand to my high school basketball coach. My moments of religious despair are a veiled selfish desire to be connected to institutions that have survived history. My desire to have faith is the same desire to have a trust fund, to be safe and stop worrying about it; if You exist, You'd understand. I'm not a bad person. Missing the last ten years of Mass and breaking every Commandment except number five on a daily basis doesn't make me a bad person. You can be good without following the church. There are five and a half billion people on this earth who have never even stepped inside a church. That's a shitload of people in Hell. Just being pretty good should be good enough. Why does Lincoln's "I feel good when I do good things. I feel bad when I do bad" make so much more sense?

Were they carrying the house effortlessly on their pink baby shoulders or by some elaborate rope and pulley system? Did they rest in a
small pile, like a pride of lions, a little orgy of angels? If they could fly,
they probably had superhuman strength as well, like ants toting twenty
times their body weight. Gisela was selfish and in trouble, but I could
help her. I might be a dunce. I might miss references. I know on the
outside my most obvious characteristic is my averageness. I only speak
one-and-a-half languages. But I am a prince and things larger than her
affection have been willed into existence. Everyone knows loneliness
and everyone only gets older and lonelier. If I hang in there, if we ate
a nice lunch together, with a glass of cold white wine, and walked up
here to see this?

The old woman's eyes were closed, her dry thick-fingered hands
clasped. She was either sleeping or deep in prayer. She didn't move as I
walked past, out into the sunlight.

❋ ❋ ❋

Gisela sat with her feet up on the windowsill leafing through an Italian
Vogue. The shades were half-drawn and the strong sunlight came beneath
the blind, lighting up her bare feet and shins. Marsh had his notebook
out. He was at the small desk at the foot of his bed, writing with a sepia-
inked pen. There was a bottle of Pimm's on the desk. He was drinking
the brown liquor from a bathroom water glass.

"The Croatian army has started taking Krajin back. We're leaving
tomorrow morning," he said without looking up as I walked in.

"All of us?" I looked over at Gisela who was ignoring Marsh and me.

"Me and you. I need a driver. You'll get paid."

She held the magazine above her, face tilted up to it. Her eyes looked
like small clear pools and if she were to lean forward, they'd empty.

"You need to find some Triple A batteries," he said, "change a bunch of this money, and maybe write a letter to your parents or whomever. Let someone know where you are."

"What about her?" I asked. She pretended to not be listening.

"She's going to look into her adoption stuff. We'll be back by Sunday. She'll be all right."

"This is okay?" I asked her.

She finished the sentence she pretended to be reading. (There was no way she knew Italian.) She looked up. "What's that?"

"Is this cool with you?"

"No. It's not."

"Anthony, I can get a local, but I'd rather pay you. You'll just be driving. This will be good material. I promise."

"You two big guys do what you need to do."

"Why can't she come?"

"She doesn't want to."

"I don't?"

"Gisela, don't be a cunt. I need him to drive me. We'll be back in three days tops. But we've got to go tomorrow. It's already started."

Gisela licked a fingertip and turned another page of the magazine without looking at it. "Well, you go do whatever it is you need to do." Then she shut the magazine, took her feet down from the windowsill, and turned to me: "You're on your own back in Budapest."

"We'll be back on Sunday."

She ignored me and walked out, letting the door slam behind her. The drapes rustled as the air in the room sucked out.

Marsh sat down on the floor and unfolded a map. "Or Monday, definitely Wednesday at the latest."

"Dude, why can't she come?"

"You need to get your batteries." Marsh began writing notes on one area of the largest map. He looked up. "These were printed one year ago and are already outdated."

"Marsh, what the fuck is your problem?"

"Northern Bosnia or Southern Croatia. Depends on who you ask."

I walked across the room and stood over him looking at but not trying to read his handwriting. I had the urge to spit into his thinning hair. Or kind of sit down on his back. Maybe pin him down and punch him in the face a few times. I began to reach out and then stopped and went into the bathroom.

"Whichever it is, we're going tomorrow," he called in.

Despite all the sun, I looked pale and porous in the mirror. My forehead was disturbingly shiny. I hadn't had a haircut since I got to Eastern Europe. There was a story in Budapest about an American going into the barber and saying he wanted only "a little" cut off. *Kiczet*. But the barber had interpreted this as leave only "a little" and he had taken a razor to the guy's scalp. My hair was now floppy. I looked like a Dutch schoolboy.

I walked back into the room.

"Listen, Anthony, don't worry about her. She'll be fine."

"Did you two have sex?"

He looked up. "Honestly?"

"Honestly."

"Of course. But believe me I deeply regret it."

"Why didn't you tell me?"

"I did, essentially."

"No, you didn't."

"It was nothing personal against you. She basically raped me the first night down in Pécs. But believe me, chap, I'm done. She's all yours. Crazy bird. Bit of a drug problem too. It was a big mistake. Plus I love Babette."

"You're such an asshole."

"Tell me something I don't know. Are you coming or not?"

He looked back at the maps. Thirty seconds or so passed: "Are you serious about this? Are you worried about getting hurt? Because you won't. This won't be dangerous. Or are you really worried about this woman? Anthony, believe me, she's fine. She can take care of herself. She obviously isn't too concerned about you."

"Couldn't I drop you off and then pick you up later?"

"That won't work. For a hundred reasons."

"She's not a junkie."

"You know what, Anthony? Do whatever you need to do. Seriously, I don't give a shit. I'll find a local. I think you're pathetic. But who cares what I think?"

I lay down on the bed and closed my eyes. He folded and unfolded the maps, like a child sifting through Christmas paper wrappings looking for one last gift.

"What would Christ do?" I said.

"He wouldn't have gotten involved with her in the first place."

"What is that feeling of just feeling like you're completely not being who you are?"

"In England we call it being American. Acting phony. Being crap."

I folded my arms across my chest. He stuck his head up from the floor. "You're not in love," he said matter-of-factly. "We should go out tonight and get you laid."

"I'm *in* something," I said. "I know you think it's retarded. But I just feel something, with her, heavy, you know, something big, something that I've got to follow, check out."

"You need to *check out* getting your knob sucked by someone other than her."

I didn't answer.

He knelt up straight. "You know what, Anthony?"

"What?"

"You're going to let this fuck you up. And I don't know if I can allow that. It's not that big a deal. Nothing is. You fuck yourself up by thinking stuff is bigger than it is. People like her are the reason no one ever gets anything done. They smash things up and then retreat into their beauty. Everyone else sits around picking up their mess." He reached up to the desk and grabbed the Pimm's bottle. I heard him pour more into his glass. "Anthony, do you think I'm a fuckup?"

He was twenty-four. Millions of people must have seen his stories. He claimed Boutros-Ghali had recently cited him in a *Herald Tribune* editorial. "Not in any remarkable way," I said.

"Because there's no difference between me and you except that I concentrate on things that matter. I have a balance. And on one scale are the things that matter and on the other are the things that don't, and do you know how much time the things that don't matter get? There are real people, serious characters on one hand, and then on the other, just plain characters."

"Also I don't fuck your girlfriends."

"Plain characters don't get a fucking second. And that woman, that messed-up slinky woman, doesn't matter, I'm telling you, she doesn't. And if you are ever going to get your shit together, you need to stop thinking about people like that. You need to surround yourself with people who do things, who produce. You are a person who can do things. I wouldn't have given you the time of day if I didn't sense that. But you're in danger of spinning around, going in circles, until it's too late, until you get somewhere and you realize, you've done nothing. You are nothing. If I had half of what you have, I'd be even better than I am right now."

"Are you drunk?"

"A little, but I'm serious. Look at you. You're just natural. You could have almost anyone. You're light and fun, but with a little darkness underneath. They love you. You say you've got a novel back in Hungary. Eighty percent written? And you had that computer job. How did you get that?"

"You've repeatedly told me I'm an idiot."

"That's what we're supposed to say to Americans, but honestly, I'd give quite a bit to be you, be able to drive. Yankee go home, but take me with you." He laughed. "Can you believe I can't drive? Gentlemen don't drive? No, children don't drive. What the fuck? What a fuckoff shithole England is. What a fuckoff ridiculous place full of children."

"All right," I said, "calm down."

"You calm down, you stupid wanker. You don't tell me to calm down. I'm the one who tells you how to not fuck up your life. I'm giving you easy real advice that apparently no one has yet given you. You have everything, just do it, just concentrate and do something. Get all that crap out of the way and do something. It's a sin how you Americans are botching up the most incredible country the world has ever produced. We, the rest of the world, would give anything to have what you have. Yet you just take it for granted. You make stupid movies, chase stupid girls, drive stupid cars, you just botch it up."

"It's my fault you can't take a shit without thinking about it in a historical context? Can't go see a castle without knowing what famous idiot ran around naked in it? All you can do is talk and write and whine about the impoliteness of the world." I didn't know where I was going with this. I felt like there was a poetic moment to be had. I was grasping for it. "Botch it up? You're such a piece of shit." I sighed. I put my hand on my lap. "I don't know, Marsh. I don't know."

The sound of a map being aggressively folded. "It's smaller than Connecticut," he said.

"___"

"I need you to drive me, Anthony."

"I need to talk to her first."

"No, you don't."

"I just want to make sure she's okay."

"She's fine."

"She's not fine. We're ditching her. She has a job to do and I'm supposed to help her."

He didn't answer. There was a large brown watermark on the ceiling. I thought it looked like Florida. I tried to think whether Florida was bigger than Connecticut.

"Do you have an agent?" he asked.

"For what?"

"For your novel that's eighty percent written."

"No." Despite my pathetic longings about being a writer, I didn't have the faintest idea of how to connect the dots between writing a book and publishing one.

"If you do this for me," he said, "I'll give my agent your book."

I pushed myself up on my elbows.

"I have a book deal about this war. I'll talk to her about your novel. Is it readable?"

"Oh, yeah, definitely. It's basically done."

"Well, do this for me and I'll get it in front of her."

I had the thirty-two pages about a band with rabies. I had the beginnings of five or six stories that all starred a guy starving and feeling kind of bleak while standing next to the Danube. I racked my brain. Had I read anywhere of people making a writing career exclusively on hope and eagerness? But wouldn't this be a coup d'état? Wouldn't this show Claire?

"Would you really?" I asked.

"If you get me to Knin and it's even remotely readable, I'll give it to her."

{eleven}

Dinner on the veranda of an empty restaurant a few doors down from the hotel. The sky a soft fading blue, and the moon already up, punching a pale tissuey hole in the awning. For a fixed price of around four American dollars, the three of us ate scampi the size of bananas, corn, baby clam risotto, and crusty bread and drank endless carafes of white wine. With the exception of pizza the night before and the occasional Wendy's cheeseburger back in Budapest, it was the first non-Hungarian food I had eaten in two months. All the flavors seemed amplified. A single vegetable tasted so formidable. A bite of corn and almost instantly I could feel the vitamins course through my dusty grease-lined veins. The wine was cold and came in pewter carafes covered with condensation. You had to be careful when you chewed the fresh sourdough bread or you would cut the inside of your mouth on the crust. At the end of the meal, I felt as if I were going to bound from my seat. All the Hungarian grease, the weeks of potatoes, the *palinka,* washed away.

We followed some music to a town square where a band dressed in torn and filthy tuxedos played a mix of polka and punk. Teenagers drank wine from plastic Coke bottles. We bought bottles of beer from a young boy selling them from a wheelbarrow. Christmas lights were strung about thinly leaved trees. Up by the stage, a mosh pit of people slammed and Pogoed, and occasionally a burst of aerosol on fire shot out above their heads. On the perimeter, older citizens were dancing traditional step dances. Clouds had moved in while we were eating and now beyond the rooftops the sky was the color of wine.

Marsh didn't dance. He stood with his left foot forward and his head bobbing. He was wearing his shoe-boots. He looked like something from seventies British Mod. I asked Gisela to dance. She shook her head. After a few beers I moved in on a group of teenage girls. I hoped they could spark jealousy.

"Dance?" I asked the whole group of them, in English, nodding toward the crowd. They looked at me with adolescent hatred, the hatred toward every living creature outside themselves and their friends. It occurred to me this might be the first time in my life where I was The Man.

"Dance?" the prettiest girl said sarcastically in good English. "Hmmm. I just don't know. We are having a big talk here. I don't think I want to dance." The girl had breasts and looked older than her friends. She put her finger to the side of her forehead. "Maybe Zita should dance with you?" She turned and spoke to a girl who hung the furthest back. Zita looked terrified. She clearly didn't understand English. The girl took Zita by the arm and pulled her towards me.

I looked the girl in the eye and held out my hand. She looked away, bit her under lip, then turned back and took my hand. We walked into the crowd. Her hand in mine felt weightless and clammy, an embalmed science-project frog. She kept turning and looking at me, trying to decipher if this was a joke. She wasn't ugly or pretty. She was somehow unformed, her parts hadn't fully grown into themselves. Her cheeks and chin weren't completely pronounced. Her body didn't reveal a character, a person, just anxiety and a heartbeat. But occasionally she smiled at me like I was absurd, like she might be the shy one, but I was the fool who thought I'd get somewhere just coasting on my foreignness.

We started in the middle of the crowd, dancing fast to a Klezmer song, but I guess she didn't enjoy me yanking on her arms like that, and she pulled me off to the side and, holding me by the biceps, tried to lead me through the basic steps of a four-hundred-year-old dance. The more you think about dancing, the more you suck at it. We ended up doing a sped-up box step, the one dance I still remembered from the class in junior high.

At the end of the set, I offered to buy her a beer. She accepted a Coke. When I asked her about La Conception, she nodded, saying "Yes, yes," like it existed, but looked perplexed, like she couldn't tell what I could want with the place. After our drinks, after we exhausted all the sign language ways of making a jackass of yourself, she pointed over to her friends and started toward them. I couldn't tell if she was inviting me. I followed her.

"Yes, we know about it," the breasty mean girl said.

"Would you like to go with my friends and me?" I pointed over to Marsh and Gisela. Gisela was hugging herself and swaying to the band. Marsh, who had been watching us with interest, waved back. I felt myself smile, thinking he looked like a putz.

When she translated for the other girls, they broke into hard, fake laughter.

"You don't want to go there," she told me. "Come with us to the beach."

"It's not good?"

"The people are not nice. I can get in, but they can't."

"Not nice" sounded all right. "Let me ask my friends," I said.

I tried to tell Zita I'd be right back. She thought I was thanking her. She smiled and mimed relief, rolling her eyes and wiping the back of her hand across her brow, like she had lived through something. It was incredibly sweet. I wanted to hug her and tell her that as time passed the difference in our age and language would mean less and less. I wanted to tell her I had a great job back in the States. I had to stop myself from leaning over and kissing her. I finally just stuck out my hand to shake. She shook and they all laughed and it seemed like it was fine.

Marsh and Gisela were opening their first pack of Yugoslavian cigarettes. I had done my charitable deed for the evening. Gisela laughed out loud, scoffing, when I asked if they wanted to go to the beach.

❖ ❖ ❖

La Conception was designed in a Mother-of-God motif. Creepy life-sized statues of Mary stood in every corner. Cisterns full of plastic colored rosaries stood throughout the club. Mirrors lined the ceiling and walls. People scooped the rosaries up and wore them like Mardi Gras beads. Waitresses wore habits and black clingy robes that opened in the front as they walked and revealed silver thongs and bikini tops and knee-high white boots. Out on the floor, wanna-be models danced with wanna-be mafia.

We hadn't connected the name with the Immaculate Conception. Now Marsh and I were falling over our drunk selves to exclaim how brilliant it was. But even as we were sharing our enthusiasm, there was the awkward embarrassment of drinking in what was basically a theme bar.

Thomas saw us and came over. His hair was yellow in the lights. He wore brown corduroys and a loose billowy cotton shirt, which made me think of Spain. He greeted us warmly, like we were friends. I felt potent; I was our connection to this sort-of local, rather than Marsh. He ordered us a round of Baptisms, mixtures of gin and white wine served in large pewter chalices. While we were waiting for the drinks, a man asked Gisela to dance.

She shrugged at Marsh and a little longer at me and then followed the man out to the dance floor, both of us watching her departing ass.

The man was trying to get her to put her arms around him. She would let him get close. She'd move her hands up toward his shoulders like she was going to pull him in, but then her palms would flatten, and she'd slowly step back and turn, making him spin her, then back to him again and step back, slowly, yet letting something bigger and better bluster up between them. A friend of his was dancing on their perimeter, showing his support, which made me happy, thinking they were idiots. When she looked over at us, the second man would look over as well. I ignored her, wanting to wait until she was in a situation she needed saving from.

Marsh ordered us another round.

"The Croatians are definitely back in it," he said. "A deal has been made with Milošević. They say they are going to take Knin back. And the Serbs are going to take Balo. Troops are at the border. It will be a slaughter." He sounded no different than my coworkers back at CNET when they spoke in earnest about optimizing database indexes and search engine algorithms. "We need to leave early."

Thomas was now out on the dance floor. He was dancing with a beautiful small dark woman who looked like a triathlete, strong and bouncy. She was tan and had bright eyes. Someone a cheeky *Maxim* article would describe as "totally fuckable." They were joke-dancing to the heavy bass of the music. Thomas was doing the Lawn Sprinkler, the Tennis Volley, and the Fisherman. They looked alive in a way I hadn't felt in years. It was easy to imagine them naked.

When I came back from taking a whiz, Gisela and her dance partner were talking to Marsh. She introduced us. His name was Dimir. He was tan and basketball-player tall and had high, defined cheekbones, making his whole face angular and wolfish. The music changed to a slow song, and Thomas and his beautiful partner came over as well.

Marsh asked Dimir if he was Croatian. He was.

"I forget, did Hungary own Croatia or Croatia own Hungary?" Marsh asked him.

"You're such a fool," Gisela said.

"Seriously, what is the word for sleeping with the enemy?"

"Does anyone want another?" I asked, holding up my empty chalice. Without waiting for an answer, I turned to the bar.

He must have seen me not having any luck with the bartender, because after a few minutes, Dimir pulled up next to me. When he smiled, it was like he possessed some mischievous knowledge that only he and I were in on. He asked me what I wanted. A beer. He yelled something at the bartender, who'd been ignoring me. Four shots and two beers came. He said the shots were *sljivivica,* a plum brandy similar to the Hungarian *palinka.* The national drinks of all these countries were from fruits no one ate and could be made under your bed.

"Is he her boyfriend?" he asked me concerning Marsh and Gisela. He spoke with a Dracula accent.

"No."

"Are you?"

"Nope."

"She said one of you was."

"It isn't me."

"She's very beautiful. Is there a problem with me dancing with her?"

I said there wasn't.

"You like Croatia?"

"Yeah, it's beautiful," I said. "I guess I didn't realize it was on the water."

"Yes, most people don't. We hope it stays a secret."

"But I guess the war is kind of fucking it up?" I said.

"Maybe," he said. "But there's always been war."

"Really?"

"Always."

"Have you fought?"

"Of course," he said, smiling.

"Like killed people and stuff?"

"*Like.*" He was making fun of me. "Of course. And *stuff.*"

"Serbs?"

"Serbs, Muslims, Montenegrins, Croatians, a few Western journalists, some children, I'll kill anything," he said. "I'd kill my mother if I could find someone else to cook like her." His mouth then broke into a wide smile. He shook his head. "I'm kidding. I love my mother very much. I'd never kill her." He stopped. In a more serious tone: "I've killed three men, all Serbs, Bosnian Serbs. They all would have killed me if they got the chance. I was in the army. What do you think about that?"

"I don't know," I said. "I'm sure it was difficult, but . . . well . . . it seems to happen. I guess I don't know. I've never been in any kind of situation that warrants killing someone." I tried to picture my fraternity brothers and me killing some guys from another fraternity. Or maybe killing a telemarketer who called during dinner. Just getting somebody and taking his life.

"But do you look at me and think, 'killer'?" he asked.

"No." I thought, tall swarthy dude dancing with my girlfriend.

"Well, you should," he said and nodded. "When you are in this country, we're all around you. Everyone here is a murderer. We've all killed. Or our fathers have killed. We are all related by murder."

"If you say so." I couldn't tell if this was some kind of threat. He seemed genuinely nice. But later I decided, and maybe this is true in all devastated places, pointing out a collective fault in your people was also accepting of humanity for what it really is: brash, violent, lusty, and murderous. Civilization isn't about voting, democracy, and "acting civilized." It's about repelling your enemy. And the rest of the world is silly with its pretenses of love and brotherhood. Your brother kills you, steals your pig, and then rapes your wife. Then he cries about it and says that if he didn't do this, you would have done it to him. Then everyone gets drunk and eats delicious banana-sized scampi.

"I don't mean to be dramatic, but. . . ." He pulled out a cigarette, lit it, took a deep drag and looked out onto the water. I thought he was joking. "America and Europe must understand: this war is not being fought by madmen, but by people like me, bartenders, students, lawyers. Citizens of this world. You know I lived in Manhattan?"

"New York."

"Two years of graduate school at NYU."

"Hmm."

"I am not some ignorant kid following orders. I've a degree in philosophy. I have studied for my higher degree in medicine. You know Hegel, Kant? You know these people?"

"I've heard of them."

"The Absolute Spirit. The real as the rational. *Ein Ding ist ein Ding*. Truth, the sublime beauty. *E'crasez l'infâme*. Yes, the Balkans are crazy. It's an endless cycle, we're running full speed at a brick wall, but it isn't a choice." He smacked the palm of his hand to the bar. His voice was rising. I looked over at the group and Thomas seemed to be keeping an eye on us. "This is who we are," he continued. "You understand?"

"I think I'm a little drunk."

"There are two hearts beating in us. We want good things. I do. I speak four languages. I'm a man of this world. Dancing and joy. Dancing is fun, no? Especially with a beautiful woman. Like the marvel of rain, of the ocean, of love between a man and woman. The world's a miracle. I know this. We should rush at beauty, demand beauty, be joyous and beautiful in life." Then he began to whisper. "But there is also a heart that beats only to fucking kill Serbs. Wants to stamp on their children. Wants *Kristallnacht* barbarity. And it's okay. I'm okay with this contradiction. I'm aware. We go on. This is just how we live. Slavs. There is no way out. And it is pompous to think there is. And I believe in Croatia. I believe in loving your county. It is a part of you. Even the poorest Americans love their country. Even while it is busy screwing them, they march, they wave flags, they die for it. Well, we are no different. I love Croatia. I believe in standing up for her freedom. At some point, you must stand up for your freedom. Without that you are nothing. Under tyranny you are not alive. You know that. That is what it means to be American. All Croatia is doing is asking for her freedom. Isn't that what America did two hundred years ago? Is Croatia any different than America?"

"How about Bosnia?" I was certifiably wasted.

"What about it?" He was pissed.

"You're asking for Bosnia's freedom too?"

"Yes, it's wrong what we did there. We never should have stooped to the level of the Serbs. But people were killed; people were wronged on every side. Shit happens. But none of it would have happened if the Serbs had let go in the first place. They are the perpetrators here."

"What should happen now?"

"The Croatians and Serbs should leave Bosnia."

"And Bosnia should be just Muslim?"

"Yes, a Muslim state. That is what they want as well."

"You know that's insane. What about the mixed marriages, what about the children of the marriages? Aren't at least fifteen percent of Bosnian marriages mixed?" Marsh had said something to this effect.

"I'm not saying it will be easy. I'm just saying it's the only solution. It's the only way to stop the killing. And it is what people want."

"*Some* people want."

"The people still alive."

"Why can't it just stop? Why can't everyone just put down their weapons and get on with their lives?"

"You really have no idea," he raised his voice again. "You just don't know. You don't know what it is to have your parents and people killed and tortured. You people are like children. There is no way you can possibly understand this. The only Americans that have any right to comment on us are the blacks. They would understand this war. But you and people like you. That reporter. You have no idea what it means to be us. Our history is struggle and war. Thousands of years. Serbs have been taking our land and killing Croats for thousands of years. You have democracy, Thomas Jefferson, Liberty Bells, the Grand Canyon; we have our mother being raped and suffocated by our nephews."

· Gisela appeared at his side. "What are you two discussing?"

"He's just telling me about Croatia."

"Sounds serious."

"Can we dance?" I asked her.

She took me by the hand. Once we were on the dance floor, I said: "That man's nuts."

"He's handsome."

"Seriously, he's crazy, he was just telling me the most fucked-up shit."

"What about your little girlfriend?" she said and smiled.

"She was crazy too, all these people are nuts. We should get out of here."

She shook her head and pulled away from me. Then came back. "That Thomas man is going to help us." Smiling. The music was picking up and she began moving with it.

"Cool," I said.

Regardless of the kind of alcohol, I, sometimes, shouldn't drink. Two drinks and I'm the biggest ass in the room or in the country the size of Connecticut. It is only every once in a while that this happens. I can't really pin down why sometimes and not others. But I started doing my splits. They are kind of my signature move. Gisela was into it. Thomas and his girlfriend came out to join us. People were moving in around us. I've been doing them since the first time I went drunk to a high school dance. I'm not particularly limber, but if I'm drunk and I just throw myself at the ground, my legs will split apart and catch me and spring me back up. I've never hurt myself, but, especially at weddings, I ruin whatever pants I'm wearing. It is kind of addictive once I get going. Sober, the impulse would never enter my head. It isn't really the type of dance move that is called for more than once in an evening, like maybe at the climax of some song that builds and builds, but I start doing them every thirty seconds; where regular drunk people maybe do a spin, I do a split. People generally get into it. Especially the very first time they see me do one. They clap and whoop and point me out to their friends. And once that starts I can't control it. I'm just doing them over and over. Yo-yoing up and down. Thinking I'm the coolest. Trying to get other people to do them.

Somewhere in the night I told Gisela I was in love with her and that we should forget about Budapest and her job and just get a house together in Rovinj. I told her we could start a winery, maybe raise goats, and live out the rest of our lives here. I could put it on my Amex. At the time, it seemed to me like I was getting somewhere. Marsh was watching us. He had stopped drinking. He kept coming over and telling me we needed to be on the road at 7:00 AM. Finally, in a harrumph, he left.

At around three, the crowd began to thin, which to me meant more space at the bar. Thomas and the beautiful woman left. I was drinking gin-and-tonics to keep me awake. Dimir was still lingering around, but since Gisela had danced with me for most of the night, he seemed cool. I asked him if he could get blow. He smiled like he could and then invited us to a friend's bar that stayed open late.

We walked through town. The air was damp and gluey. You could smell the ocean. I tried to make mental notes of landmarks and street names. I felt super-sharp like I might secretly know karate. Gisela let me wrap my arm around her waist.

The small door with a heavy metal ring for a knocker opened up into a crowded low-ceilinged pub. There was a short bar and three tables. Beams of exposed wood lined the ceiling. The walls were covered in paintings and prints. It was past three but everyone looked like they were just starting out. The bouncer locked the door behind us and told us we couldn't leave until dawn.

Dimir lined up some more *sljivivica*. Then he brought me into the side room and pulled a joint from his small man-purse.

"Hash," he said, smiling, holding the joint up.

While we smoked, he told me how much he loved New York. You could get everything in the world, at any time of the day or night. The four-dollar tea service on the red couches of the Russian Tea Room. Every kind of person, every kind of food, every language.

Like most drunk conversation, it didn't really have any conclusions. I agreed with everything he said although I'd never spent any time in New York. He explained that the major difference between Croatians and Americans was that you couldn't be a silversmith in America. I might have told him this was flirting with genius. At one point I gave him my CNET business card.

"Can I tell you about my first time?" he asked.

"First time what?"

"I killed a Serb."

"If you want."

"It's not a confession. I tell you this with pride. Not about the killing. Killing is awful. I'm the first to admit. But it is also complicated. The most complex human act. In this way Americans are very simple."

"We have tons of murder in America."

"You have crime and serial killing. That is different. You have people killing for food or stuff, gangs which are essentially just the street version of capitalism. Capitalism on steroids. And you have killing because of psychopaths: Son of Sam, Ted Bundy, Mr. Kaczynski. You don't have revenge. You don't have war. You have hungry people and fruitcakes."

He took a drag, held it, then exhaled a huge cloud of smoke.

"I'm talking about killing someone because you passionately believe they should die. Like how I believe certain Serbs should die. I want them to die badly. I wake up wishing whole swaths of people dead. You have it too. Neighbors, brothers, sometimes you don't even know you hate them. People you've never met, but sincerely wish them dead. There are many reasons. For me, it is simply because I know what they know, what they think. And they think exactly what I think: he and his family have done awful and unforgivable things to me and my family. He should die. You understand?"

I didn't even understand the degree to which I didn't understand. He handed me the joint.

"Given some arms, given even the flimsiest reason, people will kill each other."

"I think civilization is all about stopping that," I managed, and then took the joint to my lips and tried to take a small hit, but ended up with a lungful.

"No, no, no, civilization is all about just that. People were never killed so openly, in such massive numbers until civilization. Civilization is organized murder. Collective action on our desires. You must understand this. I insist. You must understand why it is okay for me to want other people dead. Why we are just acting on our human instincts, our primal passions. Why Serbs deserve to die."

His face seemed to be getting larger. His teeth multiplying. He was beginning to look more and more like a wolf.

"Alexi. A boy." He smiled. "Maybe ten."

"A child?"

"Yep."

"Shut the fuck up."

"This one was clearly going to be a man who would kill people."

"A kid?"

"My friend Markos's little brother. Alexi. This was in 1990. I was only sixteen, a little burnout. So he must have been around eleven. That's right. Not ten. And it was the spring and my family was living way out in Gračac. This was before the Serbs took it, before they shot the animals in the Bihać zoo."

He held out his hand, wanting the joint back.

"I'm too stoned," I said, handing it to him.

He smiled, took a drag and started talking before he exhaled: "Milošević rejected our declaration of independence from Yugoslavia." Then he started coughing and laughing. He tried saying it again. "Milošević rejected our declaration of independence from Yugoslavia." He was able to say it more clearly, but it made him crack up even more. I was laughing too. Finally, after getting his breath back: "And the army coming was inevitable." But this just got him laughing again. His body shaking with giggles. "And everything started to be talked about again," he said. Ha, ha, ha. He took another drag. "With Tito, nationalism was illegal," he said, his chest full of smoke. He exhaled, filling the little room. "You didn't talk about who was a Serb and who was a Croat. And although the capital was Belgrade, Tito was Croatian and all the states were equal. Right?"

I shrugged.

"And people just knew that if we talked about the past, about what had happened during World War II, then the whole charade would collapse." He stopped and held the joint up between us, lifted his eyebrows, and nodded. "Good shit." Then he was cracking up. When he could finally breathe, he opened and closed his mouth and tried to swallow. "Do you want another drink?"

"I need some water," I said. He licked his fingers, pinched out the joint, and put it in his shirt pocket. We walked over to the door leading to the main room. Gisela was talking to some French guy. She waved to us and made a face; I couldn't tell if she was mimicking boredom or sleep. I followed Dimir to the bar, and he shook his head like he was trying to get rid of the giggles and started again: "Anyway with Tito and Communism gone and Slovenia getting her freedom, it was assumed we would get ours as well. Right? We are the richest country. We aren't Orthodox. We have our own language and alphabet. We have this beautiful coastline. We have the best hash in the motherfucking world. Why would we want to be part of some stupid Federation? What are we, Star Trek?"

I pulled a stool over because my knees kept buckling and my feet felt far away.

"I would hear on my way home from school how Tibor was really living on So-and-so's farm because So-and-so's grandparents had turned Tibor's grandparents over to the Nazis and So-and-so was given their farm in retribution. After World War II, there were many horrible things done by the Serbs to the Croats because they were told that the Croats had tried to give them to the Nazis with the Gypsies and Jews. This wasn't true. Very few Croats worked with the Nazis. And few Serbs were deported." Then he started laughing again. "Actually," he said, "I have no fucking idea. But regardless, what I'm getting at is that no one talked freely about what had been done to whom by whom until the Communists were gone after '89. You know?"

I nodded like I did. I also thought about grabbing him by the wrist and begging him to stop.

"And then it slowly became okay, right? At school, some kid would come in and at lunch say that his father had been studying to be a lawyer, but then the scholarship was pulled. He wouldn't say why, at first, but a week later there would be some kind of fight between him and a child who was Serb and the Croat would blurt out in anger that the Serb was the reason he had no money or that his dad had to work in a shoe shop. You know? Or that he was the reason the kid, himself, wasn't going to get to go to the university because everyone knows that Serbs keep all the state scholarship money for themselves. So why even try to do well in school? All these kinds of little scenes happened more and more. And we were just kids, you know? And like all kids our friendships and alliances shifted almost daily. I would spend a Saturday afternoon with one kid and then suddenly he was my best friend. This was always happening, but slowly over the course of a year or two, it got so that all my friends, except Markos, were Croats. We didn't get together and talk bad about the Serbs. And when Markos was around, it wasn't like we acted any different. But we were. We were different."

"How?" I asked. I looked at us in the mirror behind the bar. His eyes were merging into one and his teeth growing.

"Oh, come on. How?" he scoffed. "We are all so uncomfortable with our past. And so stuck in it. There is no way out. Joyce was right. It's a nightmare. Americans believe that they are peace-loving and somehow morally better than the rest of the world because they don't fight ethnic or religious wars. Ha! The only difference between you and the rest of us is that you don't have a past. It isn't that you embraced some ideal that is too complicated for us. It is that you don't have a past; you made such quick work of the Native Americans. And you don't have an ethnicity, a religion. And not by choice, by pure luck. You are what? A hundred years old, three hundred years old? That is nothing. But give it time. You'll do it. You'll fight a religious war. Your luck will run out. Just wait. A big stupid country like yours. You will be in it for years, centuries. Letting your children go and kill and be killed for something that was started generations before they were even born. You'll see. You'll grow up. Become a real country with a real history. And real enemies." Then he started coughing again. It went on and on. He finally stood up and pounded himself on the chest. When he caught his breath, he took out his cigarettes. He offered me one. Once we lit them, he continued: "There are millions of people in countries with histories who have done what I'm about to tell you to their opposing group."

With his tongue, he swiped pieces of tobacco from his big teeth, pushing them onto his top lip. In little pfft's, he spit them away.

"I've gotten off track again. What I want to tell you is the story about Markos and that little brother."

The bartender arrived with two beers and a glass of water.

"This little brother was crazy. He would do anything. Markos was nuts, but not like the little brother. Neither was particularly big, but you would never want to fight them. You know those kinds of kids? Little people who would never, ever give up in a fight. You would rather fight your own father than fight them because you knew that they were insane enough to never give up and even if they did give up, they would eventually get you back."

In Skaneateles, we'd had Chad Johanson, a hyperactive psychopath who spent his formative years setting things afire. His masterpiece performance was throwing a Molotov cocktail from our dock at a raft where a dozen ducks thought it was safe to rest. They took flight on fire and soon fell from the sky in drips.

"I know those kids," I said.

"Well, there is a game over here called *Igra Strijeljaj Me,* which in English means 'The Shoot Me Game.' And although we had never seen it played, we grew up hearing stories. The gist of the game is that two people put bulletproof vests on and shoot one another. It's mainly a game played between drunk men." Then he looked at me and laughed. "Me and you?" He pointed at himself and then me.

I smiled and shook my head. My whole body swayed.

"Anyway, one day we found a pile of army equipment in the fields by our village. There were no real guns, but there were supplies like canned meals, ammunition, tents and . . . bulletproof vests.

"We quickly opened and ate the freeze-dried rations and tried to get the bullets to fire by hitting them with rocks. But this was only fun for so long. And someone suggested *Igra Strijeljaj Me.*"

"The Shoot Me Game?"

"Yeah, and we liked this idea, and Markos's little brother said their dad had a gun. At first Markos denied this. But the more he denied it, the more the younger brother assured us there was one hidden on top of the large cabinet in their dining room, and that he had taken it down many times with and without Markos.

"My friend was squirming in front of all his friends, who were now chumming up to his little brother. And as this little brother got more and more confident, he became more aggressive with Markos. Calling him names, telling him not to be such a dick-licker. But Markos couldn't do anything. It wasn't that he was a pussy, but he wasn't an animal like this little brother. He was basically a nice guy. I often think of him. I often think I would like to talk to him about what has happened to our country. He is a Serb I could talk to about all this." Then Dimir held up his hands, like *Oh, what can you do?* "So anyway, we finally decided we were going to go get their gun. We all followed them back to their place where Alexi runs inside and comes back out with an old Makarov. There were many of them left over from World War II." He stopped and thought for a second. "But now all our guns are Russian. Or Israeli.

"Anyway, we marched back through the fields, and were going to draw sticks to see who would shoot who, but then the younger brother volunteered himself and his brother to shoot one another first."

Dimir paused, waiting for me to say something. I wasn't sure if I misunderstood. Then he started laughing. "But Markos wasn't up for this, you know!" Still laughing. "You know?"

"Markos was no dipshit. And we could all tell that this was going too far, but the little brother was just a fucker. He just turned evil. He was a Serb and he was going to show everyone that Serbs are brave and Croats are chickenshit. He was going to push everyone, especially his brother, to a limit. And this is the evil I'm talking about. I don't like it, but I know it is in all of us. This is why our war will continue because I know there will always be Serbs with this in them, just like I know it is within me. And you when you're honest with yourself. It's there in all of us." He took the beer to his lips and downed half of it.

"When we got to the stash of stuff, the little brother said he'd get shot first. I had picked up one of the vests and was feeling it, trying to understand how it would stop speeding metal. There was just no fucking way, you know? The little brother asked me to help him into it. As I moved my fingers over the plastic & mesh–covered metal, I knew that

something was missing, some part or that it was defective. I just knew
the thing in my hands wasn't going to protect a human being from a bullet. And it occurred to me to say, 'Stop.' They would have listened to me.
I was very tall, even then. But I didn't. In fact when I first tried to help
the little brother into the vest, I let him put the jacket on backwards. The
zipper was on the back. I had turned the coat around so the zipper was in
the front; the largest plate of padding was in the back. But he figured this
out before he was going to get shot." He drained the rest of his beer and
swished it around in his mouth like mouthwash, then swallowed.

"When he finally had it on, it was much too big. It hung from him
like a dress. Markos looked at me as he was lining his brother up two
feet away. We had decided he should shoot from very close so as to make
sure that he only hit the vest. Markos looked right at me and I nodded,
knowing that the kid was toast. And while I was nodding, I was thinking,
'Fuck this stupid Serb. Fuck this little asshole.' I wasn't thinking about
Markos. I wasn't thinking maybe the little brother would be all right. It
was after all a bulletproof vest. It was made to stop bullets and this gun
must have been forty years old. How could the vest not stop a forty-
year-old bullet? No, I was thinking, 'And good riddance. Sayonara.
Bye-bye, Serb.' I couldn't get it out of my head. I couldn't get the 'Serb'
part out of my head. And to be honest, I had never really thought about
any of that too much before. As I said, it had come up, but I had never
really thought, Serbs should die. Or that Serbs should get out of Croatia.
But in that long minute before Markos shot and crushed his brother's
rib cage, puncturing both his lungs, all I could think was that this stupid
little Serb should die, and I looked at Markos and said, 'It will be fine.
Just shoot.'"

Dimir looked at the reef of bottles from under the bar that reflected
on the mirror, then his eyes met mine in the mirror. He shook his head,
cracking up.

"So, that is what happened," he said. "You think that is bad? Do you think I'm a bad person?"

"You let him shoot his brother?"

"From two feet away. Obviously the little brother kind of asked for it. I greased the wheels that were already in motion. But Markos would have stopped if it weren't for me."

Gisela and the French guy came over. She leaned against me. I ignored her and she pulled away after a minute to let Dimir and me finish. Once she and the French guy were talking again, he said: "Have I scared you? This isn't exactly what they mean when they say, 'A war isn't a war until a brother kills a brother.' But it is pretty good. No?"

"Kids do stupid things all the time. Pennies on train tracks. Hide in refrigerators. The kid was an asshole. Not Serbian. You really don't think you would have done the same thing if he was Croat?" I was unsure for a second if I got my nationalities right.

"Maybe, but I wouldn't be glad about it, like I am today." He smiled.

The French guy said something to Gisela in French. They were a few feet behind us. Dimir's smile changed to something less wicked, and he turned and answered in French. Then all three of them were laughing and talking in French. I listened and watched them through the mirror. I didn't understand a thing, but thought I kept hearing the English word *skateboard*. I wondered if Dimir was telling them the Alexi story. I drank the glass of water and had the confidence to stand and join them. When I did, I immediately had to reach for Gisela's arm. She looked briefly out of the corner of her eye but stayed focused on the conversation. I moved my hand to her elbow.

"You should go home with him," I whispered in her ear.

She ignored this.

"If I was being hit on by tall, tan, foreign women, I would want you to tell me to go home with them."

She must have made some kind of face, because the French guy stopped his story. She turned to me. "You need to stop drinking."

"I'm stoned," I said.

She shook her head and looked back at the guy.

I stepped from their circle and steered her away by the elbow. She let herself come with me. "I'm serious. Don't you just want everyone to always have everything?"

"Not if it means I don't get what I want."

"That's not what I'm saying. I still want you. I just don't want you not to have everything."

"You want me to go home with you and them? At once."

"No, just them, then me. Or the other way around. I don't really care. I just want you to have everything." The image of five faceless naked beefcakes with dicks down to their knees standing in a circle around the naked lithe Gisela, and me, slightly behind the beefcakes, peeking over a shoulder.

"No, it's pretty textbook."

"That's not it," I said. "I'm serious. You're not understanding me. I want you to have everything. I want you to have what you want. I want this to be all about goodness, about unselfishness. I would never want to be the thing that stops you from getting what you want."

"Go home," she said. "You're drunk." She turned and kept speaking French with Dimir and the French guy.

I spaced out for a few minutes, stretching my face and looking at myself in the mirror. But they wouldn't stop speaking French. Then I remembered a French joke.

I stepped back into their circle. "Why do the French line their boulevards with trees?" I butted in.

They shook their heads.

"So the Germans can march in the shade."

The international response was polite embarrassment.

I grabbed her by the elbow again. "Can we talk for a second?" She let me pull her into a corner. I kissed her. There was nothing. I kissed her again hard. I put my hand on the small of her back. She closed her eyes and pressed her body into mine. Then she stepped away so we were only attached by our mouths, and she delicately drew her fingers down my chest to my abdomen, then pushed the back of her hand against my crotch. I was almost too happy to kiss because I was smiling too much. I pulled my right hand between us and ran it over her great little tits. Perfect little cups of flesh. Little Porsches. I put my hand under her right one and felt its delicate beautiful weight and lifted it lightly and then I put my lips back to hers. Hovering around her, like drinking from a stream without your hands, balancing delicately, straining to stay in this perfect position. She finally put her hands on my chest and pushed off.

"Okay, okay . . . ," she said.

"It needed to be done."

"Can I still go home with one of them?"

"Yeah, of course. I just felt I needed to do that."

"You probably did." She smiled.

❊❊❊

The lights smeared. We stumbled along, our fingers intertwined, until I spotted a doorway and veered her in, and kissed her until she started laughing and held me off and, in the coming light of dawn, she looked me in the eyes.

"Don't go with Marsh," she said.

"I have to. He can't drive."

"That's not why you're going."

"We'll be back on Sunday."

"You're going because you think I slept with him."

"That makes no sense."

"You want to show him you're above it. When you're not."

"I want to see it. Did you know that rich people used to pack picnics and go watch the battles during the American Civil War?"

From behind us, a girl said my name. With one arm still around Gisela, I pulled back and turned. Four of the teenagers from the town plaza were standing a few feet from us. They looked so small and childish. Zita stood in the back and wouldn't look at me.

"You found La Conception?" the mean girl asked.

"Oh, hey. Yeah, we found it."

"It wasn't good, no?"

"It was okay."

"Did you find this Protestant there?"

"Protestant?"

"You don't like Zita? You need to pay for this woman? Should I tell Zita you aren't in love with her anymore?"

"What are you talking about?"

The lead girl turned and said something to them in Croatian. Zita, the sweet unformed teenager, stepped forward and spit on me. I flinched, turning my head away and felt it hit my ear. I wiped and my inner ear made a sucking noise. Then two or three others spat on us. Gisela shrieked and wriggled from my arm. She looked at me, and then them. "Deal with this," she said to me and marched away.

"You like her better than Zita. That girl is ugly. American girls are fat."

"She's Hungarian. I can't believe you just spit on us?"

Zita cleared her throat, like she was going to do it again. I held up my hands. "Okay, okay," I said. Zita smiled and shook her head, like it was just a joke, and she swallowed. We all stood there for a second waiting for someone to make the next move. Then Zita, in a quick motion, lifted her shirt up in front of her face, showing a pale tummy and black bra, "Whoo!" she said. They all laughed and they all did it. "Whoo! Whoo!"

They were laughing hysterically and started back down the way we had come, the mean girl and Zita with their arms around one another. Their shadows, cast by the rising dawn, pitched in front of them. I turned. Gisela was a few blocks up. Then I heard footsteps. I turned. It was one of the other girls. She was out of breath.

"We were kidding. We're drunk. Tell your girlfriend we're sorry."

Dawn was fully up as Gisela and I walked along the road to our hotel. Workmen in red jumpsuits were gathering at the café. A bread truck made its way along the road, stopping at each restaurant and grocer, leaving large bundles of bread in front of the unopened shops. Birds pierced the morning with loud electric-sounding chirps.

"What the fuck was that?"

"That's the girl I danced with. I don't know. They're just really drunk. Teenagers."

"Who spits on other people, other women? God, I've got to shower."

I put my hand on her back. With each step as we trudged up the stairs, the top of her ass touched my hand. The building was so silent; I felt we were doing something illegal. The long hall with clamshell-shaped lights mounted on the walls. Our doors were almost at the end of the hall. I only had four more doors.

"I want to put it in your ass," I said, in a breathy hesitant whisper.

She didn't turn.

"I just want to fuck you so hard," I said louder.

She stopped in front of my door.

"I'll see you in the morning," she said.

"Are you sure?" I leaned on the casing of my door, inching us both closer to hers.

"Stop in before you leave."

"You want me to stay over? We don't have to do anything." I reached up to touch her breast. She swatted it away.

"I've got to shower. Ugh."

"They were just drunk kids. They didn't mean anything."

"I still have to wash it off."

I tried to catch her eyes, but she just stared at the rug.

"Yeah," I finally said. "But get me if you can't sleep." I went to kiss her cheek. She looked up, disarming me. I lifted my left arm to touch her. I don't know if I was reaching for a hand or to caress a cheek but she flinched and turned her face to the wall.

We stood there like this. Her nose slightly brushing the wall.

"What were you feeling today?" I asked. "After we saw those people at the beach? I mean I know you felt 'sad,' but what does that mean? I'm worried that I can't feel for other people. I'm worried that all my feelings are about trying to figure out what other people are feeling so that I can act like that's the way I feel. I'm worried that I don't genuinely feel anything. Or even that I don't feel with enough imagination? Perhaps don't try hard enough?"

"I feel I have to go to bed. I'll see you tomorrow."

She went in and when I heard her struggling with the chain on the door my heart raced thinking she was trying to reopen it instead of lock it more securely.

{twelve}

Small green and red blotches. Dry heat. Bright light seeping through my eyelids. It seemed late morning. The inside of my knees burned. Then: a bar covered in empty glasses; thigh-high boots of the waitresses; talk of New York like I knew what I was saying; we had kissed. A door slamming shut. *Put it in your ass?* One side of the sheet was tucked into the bed and during the few hours of sleep I had curled the loose side underneath me. I was wrapped. My right arm wouldn't move. The top edge of the sheet taut against my cheek. Licking the edge of the sheet to scrape off whatever was coating my tongue, the tip of which felt like it had been sliced by paper cuts. I tried to open my eyes. The tendons seemed thinned and weak. A salty crust had cemented the lids shut. Scabbed over. Thing I could do partially blind: A glass of water anywhere near the bed? In small splashes: the spitting, her flinch, again the door shutting. Something again hitting my forehead.

I unpinched my arm from between my body and the sheet. My eyes still closed, my hand swept along the bed, searching for her, until it reached the edge. I tried again to open my eyes. My head swam.

A metallic ring hummed deep in the back of my head. My eardrums hurt. I began to pass out, not into sleep, but unconsciousness. The something was wet. My eyes opened. Marsh was standing there. He had a glass of water and was pouring it on me in drips. I pulled the sheets up over my head and sat in the mini-tent for a minute or so. The whole glass of water landed on me. I twisted until I almost passed out again from the exertion. Finally, I wiggled free and pulled the wet sheets down. I licked my tongue across my teeth. Marsh was still standing above me.

"Let's go."

I sat up. He handed me two Dolantin from his emergency medical kit. I went into the bathroom. My hands were swollen. My fingers lacked sensation, as if I had been working for days with sandpaper. Hives were surfacing on the bottoms of my feet. I put my mouth down to the faucet and drank and drank and drank until I could feel water sloshing in my belly. As I peed, filling the bowl up with dark orange, the pressure on my brain seemed to let up slightly. I took the Dolantin. I put a shirt on. I told him not to talk to me. I went next door. I knocked for a minute. I said her name. I stood there, tracing the embroidered wallpaper, taking short breaths, until my head stopped swimming. I knocked louder. I leaned against the door and tested the handle. I went back into our room.

"Okay," I said.

❀ ❀ ❀

We drove south on E65, the main highway along the coast. The ride was quiet for most of the trip. The Dolantin was smothering my hangover. I don't remember any scenery. I remember trying to remember to breathe. I remember occasionally we'd pass a large commercial truck with Austrian plates, and that occasionally a black Mercedes, going well over a hundred, would glide by us. After the Zadar exit, Marsh suggested we stop and eat and get water in Sibenik before starting east towards Knin. It was around eleven o'clock.

"This town was shelled in '91," he said as we circled a roundabout.

The buildings showed no visible damage from the bombing. It just looked poorer and a little more run down, more industrial than the coastal towns up north. But in the center of town there was nowhere to eat. No cafés in the streets. No pizzerias. The bombing had been over three years ago, but silent anger still sat in the city. We asked a middle-aged man on a bike for a place to eat. He shook his head and kept riding. After ten minutes of driving around, we settled on an ice-cream window that also had a selection of small sandwiches.

Marsh sat cross-legged on the grass. I sat on the hood of the Trabant.

"The city is completely knackered," he said. "The only thing the Yugoslav army succeeded in destroying was the fuckoff aluminum factory, which employed almost everyone."

"Why would an army shell its own cities?"

"Why did your man Sherman burn the South?"

"That was like one hundred and fifty years ago. And they had slaves," I said.

"I bet a lot of your Southerners don't think that was so long ago? And they certainly don't think it was about slavery. It was about federal control. Just like this." He chewed his sandwich, looking me in the eyes. "And how about the British Empire? Belfast? The Falkland Islands? People will shell anything. I understand them. What I don't understand is how the rest of the world let them do this."

Uniformed school children in white tops and gray slacks and skirts passed walking in single file.

"I hope the Serbs have run out of air. And this is the end to it," Marsh said. "This whole maneuver is purely to keep Tudjman looking good. Elections are coming soon."

"Will there be a lot of soldiers? Tanks and shit?" I asked. I had no idea who Tudjman was.

"It's probably going to be a pretty uneven fight. The Serbs are a long way from home." He pulled out a cigarette. "Didn't you say you went to college?" he asked.

"Yeah."

"European history? World history? What did they teach you?"

"I didn't really take any history."

"How did you graduate?"

"I only had to take classes in my major."

"You didn't read *Bridge on the Drina*? Ivo Andrić won the Nobel prize."

"Missed that one."

"No requirements?"

"Not Balkan history."

"This isn't Balkan history. This is the history of Western civilization, a civilization indebted to all of the Balkans for staving off the Ottomans for the past millennium. As recently as 1683 the Turks laid siege to Vienna. They were turned back, but barely, and not without the help of Croatians. Our civilization, including that cultural sinkhole, the United States, wouldn't exist if places like Croatia and the greater Balkans hadn't so generously taken it up the arse for the past one thousand years. Do I really need to tell you this?"

"Feel free to shut up anytime."

"The Italians and Austrians have used Croatia as a buffer against the Turks. No one and no one's father, and no one's father's father and so on, as far back as you could go, has known peace. If it didn't come from Italy, Hungary, or the Germans, war came from the Turks or

Serbs. We say 'nationalism' like it's a bad word, but nationalism isn't the result of a country being incredibly proud of itself. Nationalism is forged by a country being pounded on for centuries from every side imaginable. The difference between patriots and nationalists? Patriotism is supporting one's country. Nationalism is hating and fearing other countries."

He was looking at me queerly, as if I had once again mystified him with my stupidity.

"If it's nationalism, why do you always hear about Muslims?" I asked.

"You don't. You only hear about Muslims as victims. In all wars only the victims are identified by their religion.

"The media never comes out and says, three thousand Bosnian Muslims were slaughtered in broad daylight by Croatian Catholic forces. Or the town of Mostar was cleansed of Muslims by Orthodox forces.

"Catholics and Orthodox are slaughtering Muslims. As Christians did to Jews in the Second World War. That is what is happening here. But the chickenshit Western media. . . ." His voice began cracking. "Everyone is so fucking scared of religion. It's pitiful."

Sometimes I try to remember Marsh's face and can't. Even in life, it was a shifting ghostly thing. All his facial bones didn't exactly connect. Some kind of looseness. But I can always hear his voice when he really cared, a vulnerability, an openness, trying to deliver just one truth before he was gone.

We got back on a different highway, this time heading east. The map showed that Knin was only seventy kilometers inland. The wind was picking up, pressing into the row of pine trees on the left side of the highway. For a few miles we could see the sea behind us. It was white with cresting waves, but because of the distance, the waves appeared not to be moving. The sun was still high. But after we came over a knoll and the sea dropped from sight, the landscape darkened.

❖ ❖ ❖

The netting was probably fifteen feet high, and the man's body was almost at the top of it. Both his arms were caught behind him in the wire. He looked crucified upside down, suspended mid-dive. The blue ether beyond him was honeyed with bright sunlight, and his body cast a long shadow out onto the road in front of us. A few seagulls drifted around, making the sky seem that much more empty. He was the first dead person I had ever seen outside of a funeral home. My thoughts like marbles spilling out onto a floor. I thought, Murder. Cops. Electric chair. Jittery, and afraid I would lose control of the wheel. I wasn't a murderer. We weren't murderers. Marsh knows Russian. Marsh has taken a journalism-training course called "Hostile Environments." He can speak to people. Tell them we didn't put the guy up there. He was up there and we came along. Then the phrase *Total disregard for human life* started looping through my brain. It kept running. *Total disregard for human life. Total disregard for human life.* And the more it repeated, the more everything felt lighter, and the less scared I got and the more I felt that those words didn't really mean anything to me. A dumb empty phrase, which I had heard on TV shows or on the news covering anti-abortion rallies, but never said by anyone real. *A total disregard for human life. A noble sisteryard for banana stripe. A yodel blisterhard for Hunan knife.* It was just a body up on a fence. My first dead guy.

I pulled over.

"What are you doing?"

"We should do something," I said.

"Like what?"

"Like get him down from there?"

"Fuckoff dumb idea number one," he said.

"It's safe around here," I said.

"Human beings on fences. That says 'safe' to you. This is possibly the most unsafe place on earth. Forget that . . . the galaxy. The MIR space station is safer than this."

I couldn't take my eyes off it. The body looked so real; I felt for a second it must be fake. Like we were in some sort of Disney version of a war zone. If we continued around the bend in the road, we would come upon a throw-a-grenade-in-the-basket-and-win-a-stuffed-snake game. And giant furry bandits would be dancing with guns over their heads to carousel music. I didn't see how the body could have gotten up there on its own. The netting ran along the top of a small embankment on the left side of the road, probably containing someone's property. The embankment was five feet of gravel and sandy dirt. The netting was another fifteen feet. Getting up there and pulling the body down wouldn't have been very difficult. Probably just a matter of jiggling it loose. But how did they get it up there?

"It almost looks like a scarecrow."

"Yeah, Anthony, they are trying to keep the birds off the war-torn rubbish."

"Well, how did he get up there? He couldn't have gotten there on his own."

"Helicopter. The HVO throws Serbs into the town squares of villages as preliminary head-fuck tactics."

Then a crow landed on the body and started to burrow into the back of its head. Pulling out and dropping tufts of hair and scalp.

I turned the key and jiggled the Trabant into gear. As I rounded the curve, my first dead body slipped from the rearview mirror.

I began to get clammy. I wasn't nauseated, but my hands felt light and wet, like if I let up on my grip my hands would float off the steering wheel. The car filled with a warm greasy air from the vents though the heat was not on. The sun magnified through the windshield. I pushed on the toylike handle and opened my window a crack. But the gentle wind of the ocean wasn't making it this far inland. It felt as if I had opened the door of an oven.

"Anthony?"

"What?"

"We're fine, but this is a war zone. People get shot, burned, drowned, raped, and bludgeoned. One hundred and forty thousand recent corpses. Nothing about this place says 'safe.' Got it?"

"Got it," I said.

"We also don't run over tollbooth guys asking for sixty cents."

"Okay," I said.

❁ ❁ ❁

We drove in silence until we came to a sign: KNIN 34 KM. Marsh told me the town had been overrun two days before. Since then, the Cyrillic street signs had been torn down and were now in Latin lettering. The day before, Croatians moved into Balo and Ksvenic with the U.S. nod of approval, and in twenty-four hours thirty thousand to forty thousand Krajin Serb civilians had been run from their homes and were being herded south into Bosnia, which was far more unfriendly than Croatia, which obviously wasn't friendly at all.

"The Serbs will be stepping up their campaign in Bosnia. These people have to go somewhere. That joke, the Dayton Peace agreement, is over."

"Why are the Croatians doing this now?" I asked. "I thought they were officially out of the war?"

"It's the U.S. Someone must win. But your Pentagon can't back the Muslims, no one wants to back losers, especially dark-skinned losers who have ties to the Middle East. And they couldn't possibly support the Serbs, who shell crowded markets and dig mass graves, although in many ways the U.S. and NATO had been aiding them for the entire war by placing an embargo on Bosnia. That leaves the Croats. Although equally nationalistic and responsible for death camps and ethnic cleansing, et cetera . . . they are the closest to Western Europe out of all the combatants. They shared a border with Italy. They're Catholic.

"The logic is that for this to end, somebody has to win. The Bosnian Muslims aren't going to. And if the Serbs do, more mass genocide is pretty much a given. The Croats are the only choice. The U.S. has been clandestinely arming and training them. Now finally, the Croatians are taking back their land."

"Why were the Croats here in the first place? There's barely anything." I took my hand from the wheel and pointed to the area he had circled on the map he was holding in his lap.

"It doesn't seem like much, but this has always been the buffer between the coastal Croats and the Turks. It is the actual original area of 'ethnic' cleansing. These towns were the first to be hit by the Yugoslav Army in '91. Towns were designated as Serb or Croatian. Those people too old or too poor to leave were caught in the cross-fire. Entire towns flip-flopped. All the Serbs would move into one and all the Croatians would move into another. Or at least try. It took about seven months, but there was peace by the end.

"Now the Serb forces are busy down south, and they can no longer support the Krajinas. The Croats are rested and well armed. And pissed off. That's what we're going to check out: the HVO, the Croatian army, taking all that land back."

According to the map, we were driving southeast, coming up behind the frontline from the west.

❁ ❁ ❁

A small plywood hut with corrugated aluminum roofing. Sawhorses blocked the road. We slowed to a stop. Two teenagers wearing brand-new high-tops and carrying guns that kept slipping off their shoulders walked out to meet the car.

"Him, him," I pointed over to Marsh.

Marsh said a few words in Croat and Russian. And had them laughing, but they asked us to get out while they went through the car, pawing everything.

"What are they looking for?"

"They don't know."

After they were done, they went back to the hut. We got in the car.

"What's going on?"

"Killing actually only takes a few seconds," he said. "Most of war is standing around, grinding boredom, filled with the occasional few minutes of intense prayer-inducing terror. This is fine. They're just new."

"Are they in the army?"

"Probably local recruits. It's odd that they're stationed here. They usually put the younger ones up in the action." The two boys stood over by the hut talking and occasionally readjusting their guns. After ten minutes, Marsh got out and walked over, and gave them both cigarettes. Then he pulled out some bills. They took the money like it was something they'd lost and he'd found. They nodded and remained smoking, taking in the afternoon.

After the cigarette, he came back over and got in the car. The boys moved two of the sawhorses back and we drove through.

"They said that it should be 'good' today."

"Where?"

"Knin and Ksvenic. Last night the HVO moved in. They've already taken Balo."

"Are there UN troops around?"

"This isn't officially a war zone. So we'll be some of the first in the door."

"Does the rest of the world know they are doing this?"

"They do now."

❊ ❊ ❊

Furniture, camping stoves, pots and pans, lamps wrapped in sheets, all jutting out from the trunks and balancing on the roofs of small cars. And people. People on bikes. People carrying other people. Children carrying children. People carrying goats, chickens. People carrying unportable things: chairs, televisions, potted trees. A mile into the crowd: a bus, broken down and honking pointlessly. People on top of the bus. People passing notes out the windows of the bus. Everyone silent. Young men moving, like shadows, through the woods along the road. One or two would occasionally run out and meet in a whispered huddle with one of the women or older men. Marsh caught me watching them and said that young men are always in danger; their own army wants to draft them and the other army wants them dead.

In San Francisco, on the lost streets south of Market, even after the Internet companies started showing up, there were always scowling, hungry human beings begging for change, fighting over shoes or a cardboard box, but I had never seen the singular despair of a refugee, a mother lugging a child down a road, praying that yesterday, when he was quickly pushed into the back of a truck, wasn't the last time she would see her husband, telling herself that it can't be, she won't let it be, she'll see him again, she will, but if she didn't, it won't be because he's dead, it'll be because of something else, maybe he got lost, or was told that she was dead, something other than because he is dead, but for whatever reason, she'll not remember that look on his face as his hands were gripping the railing of the truck, yelling to Valetta to be the daddy while he is gone, to take care of mom, trying to be brave, but incapable of hiding his terror, his knowledge that he was a Serb and these men with guns were Croats, and Croats, even though they were Slavs—like Dimir said, they were his brothers—that they were going to be doing to him whatever might have or have been conceived to have been done to the Croats, but slightly glad that they weren't the mujahadeen, who he knew were definitely not going to waste their time doing anything other than humiliating and killing him. No, she was not going to remember this look on his face. She was going to remember him when they were young, and none of this had happened, years before, when he took her to Rab and they sat in the sand and she was wearing a new style bathing suit that she wasn't sure about and he kept telling her, and she could see it in his face, how great their lives were going to be, how beautiful she was and that with her at his side, he was going to be great, their lives, they would be great. The world was this beautiful, beautiful thing. Life was tremendous. That was the look she was going to let herself remember, just that one. But it was a luxury to think about those times; what she needed to do right now was be practical, she needed to get her children to safety.

A dullness, a worn-down exhaustion, from the constant state of total uncertainty but behind that, thoughts raced like trapped birds. The look of knowing no one gives a shit. Not to belittle the situation, it isn't in any way comparable, but I've seen the look in the waiting room of temp agencies. This look of knowing you are worth something, that you have abilities and you just need a chance to use them, while all the time sensing your efforts are useless and no one in the world cares, and you don't necessarily care for these other people in the waiting room, either. You don't want to catch what they've got. You are sure that they're capable as well, but you figure they're just unlucky. And you feel bad for them, but you certainly don't want to be contaminated by their bad luck, to catch whatever it is that got them there.

These refugees were Serbs. They were rather new to this—usually it was their enemies that were being put out and they were being put in—but no Slav was completely unfamiliar with being a refugee. All of them, Slav, Croat, Bosnian, Serb, Catholic, Muslim, Orthodox, agnostic, were from a long line of refugees, and they knew the fate of their predecessors, and it wasn't good.

I drove slowly into them. Nudging forward. The few who were walking on our side of the road kept their heads down but timidly shuffled out of the way when we got too close. As we passed, they'd glance up at us, at me, the driver, weary, with hatred and hopelessness. And you want to transmit that you're the kind of person who cares, you're just a driver here. But without action, they know you're not.

We got through and as I pushed on the gas, speeding, getting away from them, I felt as if my foot was surgically connected to the pedal and that our speed was intrinsically tied to my cowardliness, to some clump of weakness in my person.

At the outskirts of Knin I slowed. In the near distance, guns going off sounded like books being dropped. The streets were empty. Someone on a loudspeaker bleated out an untranslatable but most likely inhuman message, something like: "We don't care if you pack your things, just leave. Now!" Marsh placed a cardboard sign in the windshield that said PRESS.

"Where to?" I asked.

"Into town. Further on this road."

"Where are all the people?"

"We passed them or they're in their basements, where they've spent the better part of the last five years."

"Is there an address I should be looking for?"

"Just keep going, slowly. If we come upon someone, or anything, pull over immediately. And keep an eye out for HVO. They're our friends."

"Are we supposed to be here?"

"No one is supposed to be here. But the HVO wants us here. They see this as taking back what was theirs. They want the Croatian people to see this."

I gripped the wheel tightly as we crept along a street that seemed to be bringing us to the center of town. My car window was open. The only sound was our tires against the rubble. Storefront windows were freshly smashed, the shards of glass still gleaming.

"We should get out," he said after a few blocks. "Pull the car into this lot." There was an empty driveway next to a small home. "Take a tire off and lock it in the boot."

We quietly stepped from the car. He popped the trunk and found a jack and a wrench. I took the wrench and loosened the bolts on the left rear wheel. He jimmied the jack under the car and the back tires were off the ground. After the wheel was off, he lifted it into the trunk and slammed the hatch shut.

There were still a few more hours of summer sunlight, but we kept close to the white houses in the shade where it was chilly. Every third or fourth building had been punched with a drastic hole from shelling. Random junk lay in the street: a splayed suitcase, empty, the inside lining hanging from it in shreds as if it had been molested by wild dogs; ten or twenty empty laundry detergent boxes scattered in front of a gutted grocery store; a large gooey puddle of melted lemon gelato. The gravel stained with blood, red and brown, at different degrees of freshness. Everyone gone or too horrified to peek out.

"If you see anyone, put your hands up," Marsh finally said. "Man, woman, or child, put your hands up."

"Actively surrender?"

"Also, Anthony, if you feel the need to talk: don't. Maybe just save your opinions for something you know about, like snowboarding, or whatever it is you did in college?"

We continued walking and I followed him.

After a few minutes: "She says you didn't sleep with her. Either she's lying or you are."

He turned and looked at me incredulously, then shook his head and kept walking.

"Well, did you?"

In the distance and then quickly closer, whistling sounds filled the air. They were followed by muffled *thud thud thuds*.

"Shhh," he put his finger to his lips. He looked one way and then the other. He strained his ear into the air but the whistling had ceased. He turned to me: "If I say 'hit the ground,' hit the ground and stay down. *Do not run*. It's hard to get shot, but mortar fire . . . if you are standing up . . . if you are running, when a mortar shell hits the ground, you, anything two feet off the ground for the surrounding hundred feet will be dog food. And yes, I shagged her brains out," he said.

He waved us forward. I told myself to not follow him. I felt myself tear up and hated myself. How could I cry over this? I took some small shallow breaths. One block, then another, he began a light jog. I was too old to cry, especially about a girl. I was keeping up with him and then jogged past him. He caught up. I ran a little faster. He was running his fastest. I looked over at him and smiled and put on a small burst of speed. He stopped.

"You're such a freak," he said, huffing.

"I thought you wanted to run," I said.

We stood there, looking at one another. Then we began to hear voices. They came from somewhere off to our left. We moved closer to the buildings and slowly walked to the next street. The voices were getting louder. At the corner we peered around. There was a plaza. At the far end, there was a pizzeria full of soldiers who were drinking beer and smoking. I suddenly remembered I'd forgotten my camera in the car. Then Marsh walked out from behind the building and yelled to them. His hands in the air. One or two of them heard him. I walked out behind him. They were pointing to us. We began across the small plaza. One of the soldiers picked up a gun and fired over our heads.

"Just keep walking," Marsh said. "These are our friends."

A few of them walked out to greet us. Marsh spoke in his mix of Croat and Russian. The soldiers listened and nodded. As is often the case in foreign countries, we weren't nearly as exotic to them as they were to us.

Everyone acted serious and concerned while Marsh was talking, but eventually one of them walked out and handed us two warm beers in plastic cups. We took them and smiled and said *Hvala.* They all raised their cups. *Zivjeli!* An older man spoke to the youngest-looking soldier, who looked about seventeen. He was thin with a meekness in his eyes and lips. He had limp, dirty blond hair. His uniform was too big. His pants weren't official; they were more like pajamas. The knees were threadbare and baby pins were where a zipper was supposed to be. He was a little drunk. I couldn't help but have an underdog confidence in him.

We finished the beers and were told to follow the blond boy. He led us for a few blocks until we got to the back of a caramel-colored house with burn marks reaching up its side. The boy led us inside. We walked through an empty kitchen and down a cramped hall into a living room filled with more soldiers. A large wooden table took up the center of the room. It was covered with maps, dirty dishes, empty bottles of beer, and a half-pint of brandy. A huge man who had a mirthful grin and looked a little like Norman Mailer sat at the end of the table. He was making a list in a small notebook. He didn't look up when we entered.

"You are here to see some war," he said in a near-perfect American accent.

Marsh looked at the boy, then back at the man. "Not ideally," he replied. "We'd rather see no war. Much rather report all is well."

"I didn't think that being a peace reporter paid so well? I wouldn't want you to go away without a story."

"My readers would forgive me."

"But would they pay you? People like you make their living off people like us."

"There are always going to be enough people like you."

"And parasites like you are a rare species?"

Marsh looked away and took a big breath. He seemed to inflate. Finally: "Does the UN know you are doing this?" he asked. "Carving it up? Is Serbia taking Bosnia? Is there an agreement?"

"I don't know about any of that. We are just soldiers obeying our orders. Just reclaiming Croatian land. I don't know what their plans are for the fundamentalists."

"How many troops do you have? What did you tell the UN?" Marsh asked.

"I don't think any of that is your business." Then the man laughed. "But feel free to watch. There are still some terrorists to flush out." He stopped and spoke to the blond boy for a few minutes. He looked back to us: "You follow him, okay? He needs to stay with you if we're going to guarantee your safety."

The young blond soldier led us down an alley between two rows of townhouses. He came to a wide avenue and stopped. He put his hand behind him and signaled for us to stop too. Across the avenue we made out a clump of dark human forms and the red tips of their cigarettes. As my eyes adjusted to the gauzy light of dusk, things became more distinct: one man was kicking the wall of the building, demonstrating a part of a story. Two other soldiers watched him, laughing.

Our soldier yelled to them. He seemed to be asking them if it was safe. When they heard us, the storytelling stopped. They put up a small cheer and waved us across. They offered cigarettes when we got to them.

Inside, the house was set up like the first except there were more guns, some small metal chests, and large shoulder-firing weapons, like the bazookas G.I. Joe action figures carry. We were introduced to the men who were sitting around the three different rooms of the first floor and then led upstairs to a room on the front side of the house. Two snipers sat on milk crates, gazing into a street lit by floodlights, their guns trained on the gelato shop directly across the way. Another two were playing dominos on a small table at the back corner of the room. The snipers looked up at us for a second when we first walked in, then back into the street that the bright lights lit up like a stage.

As if for our benefit, both men started firing into the storefront. All the glass in the front of the shop had already been broken, but chairs and pieces of the counter jumped around as bullets tore into the shop. A hand was on my shoulder pulling me to the ground. After a short pause, pocking, then whizzing noises filled the air around us. I hugged the floor. I wanted to dig down into it. Plaster burst from the wall in small violent puffs. Things I couldn't see tinged. I heard the men around us chuckling. I looked up. They were smiling at one another like this was something they couldn't get enough of. The firing stopped. The two guys at the window started cracking up as well.

"There you go," Marsh whispered. "People trying to kill you. Your life is different."

We all stayed on the ground for a few more minutes. Marsh finally stood.

"Vey Cey?" he asked the soldier.

One of the soldiers playing dominos pointed him down the hall. He went in and shut the door behind him. We could hear him dictating into his tape recorder. He stayed there for an hour. I watched the dominos game. My hands were shaking. The bottoms of my feet still itched. My watch ticked louder than I had ever heard it. My vision was becoming fractal. I'd look at something and then look away and the object would hop across to where I was now looking.

They thought there were twenty to a hundred Serbs trapped in the housing project above the gelato shop. They were the last of the opposition and they were surrounded. The main Serb forces had surrendered the day before, but this group had gone renegade, and their desperation made them more dangerous. Instead of trashing the whole building, the HVO had decided to wait.

Before the sun went down, the men in the gelato shop nailed a cat. It skittered and jumped out in the street as if attached to puppet strings, before being ripped apart by a few more spurts of bullets. For the hour before darkness, they took pot shots at the mutilated body until it was just a smear of gristle and fur.

The rest of the night was silent. The blond soldier showed us to a place in the basement where we could sleep. I slumped against the back wall. We hadn't drunk any water since lunch. My head ached from dehydration and the acrid smoke. What was Gisela doing at this minute? She had earnestly not wanted me to go. I kept picturing Dimir's and that French dude's faces. Not Marsh's. Why had I left? She only slept with other people when I left. She was so much more real than Marsh and his pompous ideas about "what matters." I just needed to be with her. I could figure out how to make her love me. In high school, Asher used to say about hot girls: "Give them beer and be mean to them." When we got back, I was going to make this up to her. I was going to show her something I'd always been but just—for whatever reason— couldn't be in front of her. I was going to tell Marsh to fuck off, maybe beat him senseless. I was going to help her, take care of her lonely body, get her home.

In the morning, the men in the gelato shop shot someone in half. We heard the rustling of feet, some shouts. By the time we saw him, he was done. Taken in a flurry of gunfire and smoke. Then begging, clearly speaking to a god. Then another shot went off and he stopped, like being turned off.

Ten minutes later, more shots. A gun was trained on the dead man's midsection. It seemed like firecrackers were exploding from inside him. They fired until the midsection was almost gone, a messy magician slicing his assistant in two. He was hanging together by strings.

Marsh was looking at me; we needed to talk. I followed him outside to the back of the building. He lit a cigarette.

"This is stupid," he said. "There's nothing to report here. I need to talk to people. This isn't even a contest."

"You only cover things that aren't won?"

"This isn't news, it's just 'horror porn.' A heinous event. Slaughter. A story simply because it makes good copy. People crawling out of mass graves. Mothers being raped in front of their sons. It is the easiest war story to write, too easy." The day was warming. He was looking at the ground where he was pushing around some stones with his toe. He continued, "At some point there is no story worth writing other than the individual stories of inhumanity. People have known the politics all along. Milošević has been pretty open about everything since '89. The only real story of interest has been how well the Serbs have repeatedly tricked and used the rest of the world into helping them crush the Muslims. It's a case study of brilliant PR. A country the size of Connecticut has held all the major world powers at bay and even tricked them into aiding them. They're doing it in Srebrenica as we speak." He put his hand to his forehead and massaged his temples for a few seconds, then he stopped. "Covering this war has been a terrible career move. But sitting here watching them wait these guys out is asinine. We know what is going to happen here."

"Do you promise not to freak out if I tell you something?" I asked.

"What?"

"I forgot my camera back in the car."

He laughed. "It's not a problem. Don't worry about it."

"I need it to take pictures."

"No, you don't."

"I think I should go back and get it."

"That'd be mad."

"It will only take twenty minutes."

"Anthony, don't worry about it. You don't even really know what you're doing."

"Yeah, I do. I've been shooting a lot of pictures. I want some pictures of this. That's why I came with you."

"That's too bad. Because there's no chance. We're heading in the opposite direction. And we're leaving now. We're going to come around the other side of this building and see if the Serbs are still there."

"I can catch up to you."

"Anthony, you do not need a camera." His voice was rising.

"It will take twenty minutes."

"Jesus, Anthony. No. What is your fucking problem?"

I hadn't eaten. My throat tasted like I had fallen asleep with my mouth around the end of an exhaust pipe. I really, truly, honestly wanted to go get my camera. I could take some pictures and be a photojournalist.

"Yeah, I'll be right back."

The blond soldier saw me leaving and followed me out. He held my arm and shook his head. I shook him off and pointed back the way we came. "Car," I said. "Auto. Trabant."

He thought for a second, nodded, and motioned for me to follow him.

We weren't, but it felt like he and I were going back a different way. The streets were empty of people. They were cleaner too, like someone had come through with a power hose after the fighting. I intrinsically trusted and liked this guy. Still as we walked I found myself sizing him up. His shoulders were narrow and the pants looked so ridiculous, his eyes pale and bewildered. I had the urge to punch his arm or grab the gun hanging from his shoulder, to see if I could, as a joke.

Finally we came around a corner, and our lonely little Trabant sat exactly where we had left it. Its tire still off. No windows broken and the doors were still locked. The camera was under the seat. My eyes watered. I almost hugged the soldier. I sat in the driver seat and held the wheel.

"Okay?" the blond soldier asked me. I pressed down on the gas pedal, thinking of the highway only fifty miles west.

"Okay," I answered. I stuck out my hand. "Thanks. Thanks so much." He didn't know what I was doing. He shook and kind of laughed.

"Okay. Okay," he said and smiled.

I held up my finger. "Wait. Wait, please."

I found a pen and the rental agreement in the glove box:

Marsh,

*I'll be back tomorrow at 5 P.M. I'll meet you where we left the
car. I need to deal with Gisela. I'm only in your way.*

—Anthony

"To the journalist, okay?" The blond soldier was confused at first,
then after I repeated Marsh's name a few times, seemed to understand
and smiled at his understanding.

He watched as I took the tire from the trunk and put it back on
the car. Then I took out the map to double-check the roads. The soldier
came over and kept tracing his finger along a different route that went
north before going west again. He pointed up a road then at the route
going north.

As I was backing out: "Anthony, you naft bastard, what are you doing?" Marsh was running up the block toward the car. I took my foot off
the gas. The soldier held the note out to him. Keeping the car in gear, I
rolled the window down all the way.

"Where the fuck are you going?"

"I'm going to go check on her."

"This is my car. You fucking bastard."

"Okay, okay, chill out," I said. I put the car in first gear and began pulling back into the spot. I was going to get out and put my
knee deep in his groin. I dropped it into neutral. Then blood splashed
across the windshield, followed by the echo of gunshots. I heard
him shlump to the ground. I turned and Marsh was gone. The blond
soldier was crouched down and running into a building. Then more
gunshots, loud whap! whap! whap! and my hearing dimmed, like I
was underwater, and the car rattled and the steering wheel tugged.
I sunk into my seat, ducking my head, and stayed down until everything was still again and the only noise was the engine running. The

earth seemed to be swaying. Through an internal megaphone: "YOU
ARE CATHOLIC, CAT-TOH-LIC. YOU ONCE VOLUNTEERED TO
FEED HOMELESS PEOPLE ON THANKSGIVING." Then a kind of
salivary whistling noise right outside the car. Like a tire was deflat-
ing. I waited until there was complete silence other than the whistle
and slowly opened the door a crack, still ducked down. I could see
Marsh's hand in the dirt. I opened further and his shirt was soaked,
like he'd been hosed down with blood. His chest was moving and
the whistling noises were coming from there, but the whistling was
changing into bubbly fizzing. I pushed on the gas, inching forward, and
his face was intact but bits of skull and hair were sprayed across the
ground. A small river of blood was filing in around them. A puddle of
swelling blood. It would soon be at the tire. I pulled the door closed.
The engine was still running. I touched the gas pedal and it revved. I
put the car in reverse but kept the clutch in while I cranked the wheel.
The car quickly jacked around and I floored it.

❋ ❋ ❋

Five minutes outside of town I had to stop because three drunk men
were trying to kill a sheep. They huddled in the middle of the road. They
had a large knife but it was too dull or they were too drunk. The sheep
had dark red-brown spots all over from where they had stabbed it.

I honked. The one who was trying to cut its throat waved me away.
He was bone-thin and nearly seven feet tall. He wore a San Jose Sharks
hat and Members Only jacket. He looked vaguely like my Little League
baseball coach, Mookie McGlynn, who used to come to Saturday morning games deadly hungover and, after the lineup and our positions had
been assigned, would pull his mirror sunglasses down and fall asleep.

I waited.

The Mookie guy straddled the sheep so that the animal's head was between his legs. He pointed to its head, and made an underhand wave motion with his hand, as if to direct me through, but at the end of the wave he dramatically pointed at the sheep's head and then clapped his hands together. The sheep shuddered and bucked. He wanted me to run into the sheep's head. I revved the engine. The sheep squirmed furiously. I drove towards the man, missing the sheep's head by a few inches. I kept going.

The road went north through some newly planted fields and then everything darkened as the car entered a forest of thin young pine trees. The trees had been planted in orderly rows. The sun pitched their shadows across the road in straight lines. As I drove, my breathing synchronized with the rhythmic passing of these lines. In some places, there was a disruption; trees had been cut or blown down—and I'd hesitate and lose my rhythm and not breathe until my chest felt it would burst. After I emerged from the forest, the road cut back, west, through more fields of inch-high plants, and a few miles—only ten minutes—before I turned back onto E65, mortar shells began to fall on what looked like a deserted farmhouse. The shells were coming from a small patch of forest. I wouldn't have noticed the farm until the shells began falling around it, sending fountains of dirt up from the flat green land.

{thirteen}

I STOPPED ONCE to inspect the car—most of the blood had been on the windshield but there were three bullet holes in the trunk—and once to pee and pick up two bottles of wine. But I was back to Rijeka in under four hours. In the lobby, old men were playing cards. A younger woman stood a few feet back from their circle, smoking and watching the game. The oversized chandelier seemed to have dropped a few inches and now hung so low I was tempted to reach up and touch it. Every other bulb was blown or missing. I thought of the Salinger story where the child knows his sister has been flying in her sleep because he can see her fingerprints on the dusty light bulb hanging from the ceiling. The card players looked up, took me in, and then resumed their game. Guests who wandered in were a curious novelty but nothing of real interest.

As I was walking past, the woman stepped away from the game.

"Yes?" she asked.

"I'm going up to my room."

"You and the man were checked out."

"I'm going to see the woman."

"Are you her boyfriend too?"

"Kind of?"

"Are you going to fight?"

"Fight? No."

"You not going to have troubles. I don't want troubles. I make you leave this place with much fast if there is trouble."

"We're friends."

"Yes, yes. She has too many friends. I wouldn't have let you the room if I knew." Then she looked down at my sandals. She inspected my whole person. She didn't seem impressed. "Okay, but no trouble. I don't want any trouble. Yes?"

"Yeah, all right. Thank you."

I rested for a minute when I got to our floor, and then knocked.

"No one's home."

"It's me."

"Me who?"

I tried the handle and it gave. I opened the door slowly and stuck my head in.

"It's me, Anthony."

She was lying on the bed in a T-shirt and her panties. I stepped in before she could answer. An ashtray, a needle, and a rubber tourniquet rested on the Italian *Vogue* next to her. She was watching a German talk show with the volume off. Her pupils were gone and her irises had turned more aqua than brown. Her skin was visibly damp. Her hair uncombed and sticking to her forehead in strands. Her legs crossed at her ankles. The skin on her knees dry, but her legs were smooth and hairless. Her arms splayed out across the bed and her nipples drove tight against her shirt. Fucked up, but coherent. Coming down or going up? Who cares? I wanted to sink into her. My dick shifted off my leg. It didn't matter where she had been or with whom. I wanted to be on whatever she was on. And slide in and push up against her and sink. My logic was against the ropes. Everything in me wanted to have sex with this person. I just needed to feel something other than Marsh. Bend her over in the bathroom, her hands bracing the sink for support. In this bed, her legs holding me in. Or her on top, lazily riding. For Marsh. If we could get her the children and get her back to San Francisco, she'd let me have sex with her. We could get out of this. I told myself this wouldn't be a hate fuck. I could get the money from my parents, pay whomever, get her whatever she needed to get away from knowing these people, and then we, her and me, could get on a sailboat and go to Italy and spend the rest of the summer walking though the duomos of Venice, Florence, Siena, and Rome. Not thinking about dead journalists. Living cheaply on pastas, red wine, sex and art, having all kinds of fun hotel sex, and then she would let me have sex with her right now. Let me in there and let me stay for a few minutes. We could save each other.

"Hey."

"What are you looking at?"

"You okay?" I asked.

"Until you got here, I was feeling better than I have since the late eighties."

"What are you on?"

"What am I 'on'?"

"Where did you get it?"

Then I noticed the clothes nailed to the walls. Arms, hands, legs, feet and faces drawn in with crayon to make the clothes look attached to people. The dress she wore on the day we met Thomas on the beach hung in the stretch of wall between her bed and the bathroom. Two poorly sketched legs stuck out of it. A face coming out of the neck with lidless eyes and some scratched-in hair, manic and two-dimensional, the bad dream puppets in Mister Rogers' Land of Make Believe.

"Look at this shit," and she held up a page from the *Vogue*. A recipe with an accompanying picture.

"Are you okay?"

"What crap. 'Stuffed swordfish rolls,' *Involti di Pesce Spade*."

"Did you take his Dolantin?" I asked. The clothes might have just moved.

"What hack work. It's all dried out. There's no background food, no ambiance. Total crap."

"Did you take it all?"

She held the magazine up over her face for ten or so seconds, then pulled it back down. "Are you still here?"

"I'm in love with you," I said. "Something awful has happened."

"That's sweet, Anthony. What is Dolantin? I've never heard of it."

"We can get you out of this. We can walk away from all this and be us, go on and live great lives, you and me, together. We can go to Italy. We can Eurorail."

"What's Dolantin?"

"I'll get us out of this. But I need some help. Something has happened to Marsh."

"Seriously, quit with the 'us.' Quit with all of it. I'm so sick of Marsh, and you. You're children. Just leave me alone." I stood there. She grabbed her cigarettes and shook one out. Missing her hand, it rolled down her chest onto her stomach. Then she asked: "What is Dolantin?"

There was a three-piece suit held loosely to the wall by ten-pound nails through the shoulders, waist and ankle cuffs. And next to the suit, a blue windbreaker with jeans sticking out from the bottom.

"Basically morphine," I said. "I think it's German. Marsh carries, carried it in his first-aid kit. It's really good." My voice sounded far a way, kind of fey and breathy. "Did you talk to Thomas?" I asked.

Next to the full-length mirror, there was a long white wedding dress
tacked to the wall. Someone had drawn the face with much more detail
than the others. The bride had teeth and purple hair. Gisela noticed me
taking in the bride. "Oh, I forgot to introduce you to my other friends."

"What do you mean?"

"'What are you on?' 'What do you mean?' When did you become
such a dope?" She sucked from the cigarette and blew, watching me for
a reaction. "That's Lucy. Lucy"—and she pointed to me—"Anthony."
Then she turned toward the bathroom. "And this is my friend, Ference."
Then the large wall at the end of the room: "Those two are Mikal and
David." She waved toward the one pair of khakis tacked to the wall, above
which were two faces suspended mid-wall, unfinished friends. "These are
all my friends. After you and Sir Fuckhead ditched me."

"We didn't ditch you."

"After you left, I had a party. But I couldn't find anyone to come."

"We didn't ditch you."

"These guys here"—she waved her arm like Vanna White—"were
my only friends."

"Gisela, you're freaking me out."

She lifted her drink and toasted some of her Friend clothes.

I sat down on the corner of the bed, moving towards her. "Honey,"
I said, putting my hand on her leg, "this is ridiculous. Hurting you is so
'not me.' So against what I'm for. Seriously, I think I'm in love with you.
I want to be with you so fucking bad. I want to be together. I want to be
your boyfriend."

"Men," she said.

I crumbled toward her, almost rolling onto her, full of grief but getting my head closer to her crotch. My hand and arm pushing up her leg.
My elbow on her knee. My hand on her thigh. Kind of not, but all the
while leaning towards her crotch. Shooting for tension. I wanted the

control that regular, plain old fucking has never given me. Your tongue on her *mons Venus* has ten times the power of your stupid meat in any of her holes. Once your mouth is hovering above her, it's over. And then once that thought was up there, I couldn't get it out of my mind: heroin, German morphine, and licking her. It needed to happen, had to. It would all be great if I could get her to come. I pictured her arched. Eyes closed. Me looking up through her pubic hairs, able to see an immediate facial reaction to my tongue barely grazing her clit. I move, she moves. I twitch, I blink; she gasps, shudders. We'd move to a different hotel, pool our drugs, move on to my Italy plan. Bada-bing-bada-bang. Bada-my-tongue-on-your-clit. I leaned my head against her knee and put my lips to her dry skin. Is there something humiliating about going down on a girl? Maybe at first, with you just bobbing around down there, her up top, taking in the ceiling, wondering about postcards she meant to write, wondering whether she should start yelling out instructions, but then once you've done something to display that you have a vague idea of women's geography, once you demonstrated your ability to breathe through your nose, she's sold, she's going to sit back, relax, surrender, and let your tongue ride her little pink guy until whammo, she's a gasping, bucking, helpless fool, and you've won, and who looks silly now?, and once she catches her breath enough, so that she can just beg for it, then the dynamics have turned and those first few minutes of shame have matured into a hefty dividend. I was inside her thighs. I was in the cleft of her labia, then over it into the real, hunting for dampness. Then back up around her hairless thigh. And retreating even further to the knee. Pulling her underwear down with me. Slipping out one leg and then the other. A quick breath, gulp for air, then down again. And it was damp. The store was open. My tongue did a long pass, parting the lips, stopping for a brief, light second on the small tent of skin over her clit.

"I'd be careful," she said. "I think he came."

This is the girl who draws. A Young Pioneer. Did she laugh after she said this? My tongue stuck as if it were frozen to a chairlift bar. What would Asher do? What would a Man do? He'd make it fucking happen. He'd astonish her by forging on, blow her away. Because who fucking cares? I witnessed death. It's protein. Someone else's, but it's all just life stuff, matter forming, transforming, cells and atoms, tree bark, a worm, a fish, a Croatian guy's spunk, a dead British guy going back into the ground. Just don't swallow. She's waiting. She's not laughing. There's over a bottle of wine in me. That will kill anything. Just go on. Do it. She wouldn't have let me even begin if he had. She just hasn't showered. It's a musty taste but compared to what? I've never dined here before. And so what if he freaking did? This is your chance to show her an extraordinary love, an untouchable love, a wide and deep love. Blow her away. What was this, if it wasn't love?

"Seriously, it's kind of gross. I don't think I can let you continue."

Then I heard the door open.

{fourteen}

IN CROATIA IN 1995, you could murder, rape, steal, light things on fire. If you wanted to, you could round up a group of people, who were like you in every way except that their ancestors, not they themselves, just their ancestors, believed in a god different from your own, and you could expel those people from their homes, rape their wives, refuse to serve them at your restaurant, no . . . wait . . . , you could take their restaurant and refuse to serve them at their own restaurant. You could refuse to serve people who had served you their whole lives. You could rationalize atrocity after atrocity. But apparently you couldn't hang American-made clothes on your hotel room walls.

Two police officers stood in front of the receptionist. One officer was already well into the room. Their uniforms were a mesh of police and military. The one already in the room had a freshly shaved head and a scar running the vertical length of one cheek. I reacted slowly, an ostrich pulling its head from a hole. Before I made it all the way up, Gisela had shoved the magazine and needle underneath her, and with the astonishing speed of teenagers caught by their parents having sex, she pulled a pillow over her waist.

"This is not allowed."

"We are engaged," I said.

"Passports," the scarred one demanded.

"She didn't do it," I said. "It was me, I took the car. But I didn't shoot him."

"Passports, ID."

I shuffled backwards off the bed and went to shake their hands. "I'm Anthony Cavanaugh. How are you? I'm a journalist." He didn't know what to do with the hand and nodded to me, then Gisela.

"Both passports."

I handed him mine. "I'm a journalist," I said again. They both inspected the passport. Then the nonscarred one put it in his pocket.

They looked past me to Gisela. "Put on," the scarred one said to her. Then the taller one walked past him and started taking pictures of the Friend clothes.

"What is the problem?" Neither of them would look me in the eye. I looked at the front desk lady.

"Not allowed," she said. "You can't sell clothes."

"We weren't."

"You can't have a black market here," she said.

"We aren't selling anything."

"I saw you, and her." Gisela still hadn't said anything and hadn't really made any attempt to put on any more clothes.

"No, wait a minute. . . ." A baton came down on my collarbone. I heard it but wouldn't feel it for a few more hours.

❋❋❋

They yelled a lot. No one would look me in the eye. If I tried to talk, they squeezed my collarbone. I was placed in a small windowless room that smelled of detergent. Its bare walls were painted flat gray. The polished concrete floors shown under the bright lights. There were only two desk chairs for furniture.

I had seen *Midnight Express* a couple of times and was trying to remember how the kid in the movie messed up. Was there something he hadn't done right in the beginning? Was there some obvious thing that I should be doing? Did he know Turkish? I couldn't even remember if he had done anything illegal. If maybe he was set up. All I could remember was that he was in prison for twelve years and that his dad had come over for the trial. I tried to picture my dad in a courtroom. My thoughts were flipping between jokey ideas about sending my parents a series of postcards and the terrifying helplessness of spending time in a Croatian jail without more Dolantin.

A young cop came in and told me to take off my pants.

"What for?"

"Don't you want an exam?" But then he smiled. "It's free."

"I didn't do anything."

"Then you won't mind if I search you."

"For what? I haven't done anything."

"Then take off your pants."

"No."

"Come on. Your girlfriend liked it when I searched her."

He came across the room. I clutched onto my belt. He grabbed me by the elbow, pulled me up from the chair, and pushed me in the direction of the open door. Holding my pants, I stepped out into the main office. He pushed me again, towards a hallway. We stopped again at a metal door. He unlocked it. Once it was open, I tried to start walking, but he was too fast and shoved me extra hard for trying to get away without a push. Halfway down a row of cells, he stopped me and shoved me into an empty cell.

There is nothing quite as crushing as being deprived of physical freedom. When the possible realities began to pile up, and the pain from my
shoulder got too acute, I stood and yelled, "We weren't selling anything."
But I stopped this after someone a few cells down started mimicking me.
"Ve varnt schelling anyting." The cellblock broke out in laughter each
time. Even after I stopped, he'd let out another one, and everyone would
have a good laugh.

Later in the day, the guards shoved another man into my cell. He
was wearing a wool *djellaba* that hung loosely from his thin wiry frame.
Underneath the layers of material, his movements were deft and quick,
like he had an animal under there with him. The skin on his face and
hands was oily and dark. His hair was also dark, worn long in thick, shiny
locks. Beautiful. He had mascara or some kind of makeup around his dark
eyes that looked like Milk Duds, but this didn't make him look feminine.
It was more like war paint. He looked both ragged and dandified at the
same time. More foreign than anyone I had yet seen in Eastern Europe.

At first he was silent. He sat on his haunches, looking around like
he'd just woken up there and if he could go back to sleep he would eventually wake up safe at home. Then he stood and put his face to the bars,
got on his tippy-toes and screamed. Shrilled. In a language I had never
heard before. Nothing anyone could mimic. Not cries or begging; he was
making demands. I didn't exist while he was doing this. He didn't look
at me. He held the bars so tightly his knuckles turned white. I sat on the
metal bench, going "Hey, hey, what's up," hoping he wouldn't get us both
in trouble.

He finally stopped and laid face down on the cement floor. He
stretched his arms out in front of him like he was mid-dive and began
mumbling into the ground. He stayed there for about thirty minutes,
before he sat up, crossed his legs, and tried to talk to me. He repeated
the same line over and over, looking to me for a confirmation to his

point. "No?" he asked. I shrugged. "No?" he repeated. I held up my hands and shook my head and said, "I don't understand" in English, German, Hungarian, Italian, and French. Sometimes he found this comical; at other times he lifted his fist to punch me, and stopped at the last second and brought his fist into the palm of his other hand, like he wanted to demonstrate how hard it was for him to restrain himself from popping me.

He got tired of us not understanding one another and started doing pushups. Hundreds of them. He went on for over an hour. He did single-armed ones or sometimes threw in a clap in between. The bobbing up and down felt sexual to me. I wasn't aroused, but I felt embarrassed for having sex thoughts at all, the way gay porn can make you feel.

After the pushups he sat in the corner with his arms wrapped around his knees. "Americi?" he asked me.

"American." I pointed at my chest.

He considered this. "How come no help?" he said in pretty good English.

"Help?"

"Americi no help."

"Help what?"

"Irani help, Allah help. Americi no help. Americi help Jews. Americi no help Bosni. No help?"

"Help who?"

"Bosni dead. Bosni child dead. Why Americi no help?"

"Bosnians? It's not our war."

"What, 'It's not our war.' What is this? There is a war. Yes?"

"America wants peace. Pax. America has lots going on."

"'It's not our war.'" He mimicked me.

"We had Vietnam. You know Vietnam?"

"Irani help. Iraqi help. Saudi help. Russia help. Chini help. Americi no help Bosni bambini."

"I think Americi helps in a different way. Through the UN. The United Nations."

"Ooo. En." He huffed. Then spit on the ground.

His ranting started again. And again, it was as if he were alone in the cell. Then more pushups. After a few hundred, he calmed down and for about an hour or so prayed with imaginary beads, occasionally looking over at me out of the corner of his eye. He'd take a deep breath and then few short ones, his fingers worrying the air.

"Sponsor me in Americi," he said, after an hour.

"Sponsor?"

"I go to Americi with . . . ," and he pointed to me.

"Oh, sponsor you," I said. "Sure. You come to America with me."

❂ ❀ ❂

Guards woke us in the morning and pointed for me to follow them. When it was clear that I was going and he wasn't, the man hugged me. He smelt of spices and sweat, an odor that had clung to him for thousands of miles. While he held me, he said, "Find something to die for." I looked at him, confused for a second, not sure if he was in fact speaking English. He spoke again: "Find something in the world worth dying for. You are alive when you know what you would die for. I will die for Allah, but we all die for something. Find something as great as my Allah."

They took me down the stone hallway to a small room adjacent to the main office and sat me in a green metal chair. They put a pen and piece of paper on the table and left. I watched a clock on the wall out in the main area for an hour. Then two officers brought in a clipboard of forms. They wanted me to sign them. The forms were written in Serb-Croat. I said, No. One tried to explain that I could leave as soon as I signed the papers. I said, "I can't read this. This is all gobbledygook to me." They handcuffed me, placed the clipboard on my lap and left me alone for another hour. I hadn't eaten in twenty-four hours, my whole body quaked for water and Dolantin. My bruises itched.

Dimir walked into the station. He saw me but pretended not to. I twisted in my chair to keep facing him. When it seemed he was going to look in my direction, I meekly stood and lifted my cuffed hands.

He lifted his eyebrows and I began to stand fully, but he shook his head. Then he looked away and didn't look back and soon he followed a cop into a side office. Fifteen minutes later, he came out and one of the junior officers walked over, took the clipboard from my lap, unlocked the handcuffs, and motioned for me to stand. Dimir came in and looked at the clipboard. After a minute of reading, he handed it to me, said to sign, which I did, and we left.

"Just keep walking," Dimir said, once we were outside.

We walked down toward town. I had the jumpy fear that at any second there'd be a hand on my shoulder.

"Where's Gisela?" I asked.

"Moved to a different hotel."

"She wasn't arrested?"

"No, smart woman. Typical Hungarian."

"Are you kidding? She wasn't arrested?"

"Neither were you. If international media found they were randomly detaining Americans, it would not be good."

"But she didn't spend the night in jail?" I felt a burp of pride that my fate was somehow intricately tied into the huge hands of American foreign policy. But how had she gotten out of it?

"Maybe the room was in your name?"

It was in Marsh's.

"So how was it? Did they treat you okay?"

"I think my collarbone is fractured. And a man in my cell wanted me to sponsor him," I said. "He wasn't Croatian. He was dark, like black, dark. Maybe gypsy."

"Pakistani. I heard them talking."

I tried to visualize a map of the Middle East. At best I could identify Saudi Arabia and Israel.

"The police were very proud of the Pakistani," he continued. "A mujahadeen. Fighting for the Bosnians. They come from all over. Even America. They're the bad . . . how do you say? . . . motherfuckers and the only outside help Bosnians have. They are what happens when the world powers allow innocent people to be slaughtered; the truly wicked step up and claim moral superiority."

When we turned another corner, the bay was below us.

He continued, "He'll most likely be turned over to the Serbian army in exchange for Croatian political prisoners. He's a dead man."

I tried to imagine a life in which you would ask someone like me for help. "He told me to find something worth dying for. I guess that's from the Koran."

Dimir thought for a second, then smiled a wicked smile. "Kierkegaard. 'The point of life is to find something worth dying for.' Kierkegaard."

We passed through the square where I had danced with Zita. We had it to ourselves. There were two Roman pillars standing at the far corners of the plaza that I hadn't noticed during the night. The sun was high. The pebble ground baked white. All the people were either near the water or inside the cool dark rooms of their stone houses.

I felt airy, without substance. Things whirling. Philosophers. Holy Warriors. Croatian prisons. The wind was pressing down on the water and coming up through the streets, rocking the shop signs. An old woman sitting on an overturned bucket in the shade of an alley. The air was salty and dry. D'Annunzio. Anarchy. Babylon. Not putting anything together, but feeling connected to ideals and history, to things so much bigger than myself. Sensing a heart in the world. Hearing it vaguely, softly, beat.

"Do you know where your friend is?" he asked.

"I thought you said she was at a hotel?"

"No, the journalist, the one who went home early?" He looked me in the eyes: "Someone was killed in Knin."

"Where's that?"

"Last night. They didn't print a name."

"That's south?"

"South and inland. I saw this on the news. I don't know if Gisela knows. She left after breakfast for the Splendid. She said she had business. But your friend was very experienced, no?"

I couldn't catch my breath. I took short huffs, Lamaze-style. I told myself I was calm. I felt calm. But my body was freaking out. Blood rushed to my ears. We passed a closed camera shop. A man was sitting on the ground smoking a cigarette and drinking an orange soda. A small leafless tree, its branches like arteries. We came to a second plaza. It seemed vaguely familiar and Dimir stopped. "I'm this way," he pointed east toward the water. "She's in the Kontinental. They asked you to leave the Meteor. You don't want a drink or anything?"

I was dehydrated. "No, no thanks."

"I maybe come by tonight? Okay?"

"Yeah, of course. Thanks so much for getting me out. Do I owe you anything?"

"No. Please, my friend. There were no charges. It was nothing." He waved his hand in a grandiose manner. He was so fucking tall. I had tasted his cum. I'd gotten someone killed for her. We shook and I headed towards the Kontinental.

※ ※ ※

She had instructed the concierge to give me a key and had left a note saying to wait for her there. She'd be back by four.

Her bed was made. There were a bunch of legal documents on the
bureau. I found Marsh's and my bags in the closet. I riffled through
his bag until I found his first-aid kit and slurped down two Dolantin,
thrilled for a second that I had been stuck in jail for the night and unable to get to them, leaving that many more left. I showered, feeling
the smell of Knin and the Pakistani slide off me. There was a dick in my
dorm my freshman year in college who thought he was a philosopher. He
was constantly asking you sophomoric but slightly engaging questions:
Do you believe in abortion? Yes. *Do you believe in god?* No. *Do you think
humans are no different than animals, elephants, cows?* Yes, we're all just
animals. *So if you didn't live in a society that would lock you up, and you would
somehow be better served if I was dead, you wouldn't have a problem killing me?*
No, I'd have a problem killing you because part of our physiology is that
we sympathize with our fellow human beings. I'd feel pain because I
could intensely "suppose" what it's was like for you to be killed. And that
would be unpleasant. *Okay, but what if a baby was born into a black wooden
box and lived in the box for fifteen years, given only enough food and water to
live, but no outside contact, no human voice, no books, language, et cetera . . . And
then after fifteen years you were told you'd get a million dollars if you threw some
gas on the box and lit it, could you do it?* Ultimately I don't know anything
about mortality and morality. And I know that I don't know, and I'm
scared.

I took a pair of red corduroys out of Marsh's bag. Then while I
was looking for a shirt, I found six mini-cassette tapes in a scuffed-up
Ziploc.

❊ ❊ ❊

Most of them were back in the shade of the Splendid, around the front
door waiting for lunch. The women looked up from folding white sheets
and then away as I came down the path. The children cared less. I recognized the music as Vivaldi's *Four Seasons*. It seemed louder than when we
were last there.

In English, I asked a small group of the women for Thomas. They
looked at each other, then one nodded and indicated with her head to
follow her. We walked around the building. Gisela sat in the shade of a
small plum tree, smoking, and watching Thomas, who was shirtless and
painting the bottom of an old green dinghy.

He looked up and smiled. He tried to scratch his nose with his pinky
finger without getting paint on his face. When she saw me, panic crossed
her face.

"Enjoying your freedom?" he asked, holding his paint-covered hands
forward, demonstrating his inability to hug me.

"What happened?" I asked Gisela.

"You're okay?" she asked, but looking me in the eye and shaking her
head, no, no, no.

He bent over, put the lid on the paint, and wrapped the wet brush
in plastic.

"So how is it?"

"Okay. Have you guys heard from Marsh?"

"No. Wasn't he with you?"

"Sort of. But we had a disagreement," I said. "He told me to leave."

Thomas crouched down, poured some gasoline on his hand, and
rubbed vigorously.

"About what?" he asked.

"Nothing really, I was just in his way. He's a pretty serious guy."

The paint balled along his palms and between his fingers. He picked
at it and flicked bits to the ground.

"So Gisela and you are going to be of assistance," he said. His eyes remaining on his hand as he continued to pick at the paint. "Have you ever been to Austria?"

"I have actually. It sucks."

Another foreigner came out and said something to Thomas in a language I'd never heard. Sounded like a really drunk Englishman speaking German.

"You guys want lunch? Pickled cabbage?"

"I'm fine." But Gisela got up and began to follow him inside, so I did as well. He introduced us to some of the other workers. Most of them were Danish or Scandinavian and in their twenties. They looked like a band or a swim team. They all had long hair hanging down over their hazel blue eyes. Their cheeks were high, round, and sunburned. Ignoring my protests, Thomas put two slices of bread, a bowl of the watery soup, and a cup of red juice on a tray for each of us. We followed him to a table full of children. He ordered them to make room. We sat down.

"So this is very nice of you two." His mouth smiled, but he looked at the bread in his hands that he was tearing into small pieces.

Gisela abruptly said: "It's not a problem."

My face filled with blood. I yawned nervously.

"Why we going to Austria?" I asked.

He kept looking at his bread, then staring into his soup. Shaking his head. "These people are so messed up." He took the juice to his mouth and slipped slowly, like it was an expensive liquor.

I repeated my question. I tried to corral two small pools of shimmering grease into one spoonful. At the last instant as I lifted the spoon from the bowl, a little bit would slip over the edge of the spoon and back into the bowl.

"Anthony, I told him we'd help two of the children here."

"Cool!" I said with too much enthusiasm.

"There are some kids in trouble."

"That's great!" I said.

Thomas looked at me queerly. "These people are in trouble Anthony. There's nothing *great* about it."

"Right, but it's cool that you two are working things out."

"We're bringing them to their mom," Gisela said, giving me a look. "In Austria."

"Oh?"

I was asking her, but Thomas cut in: "These are both Croatian and Bosnian refugees. This isn't an 'ethnically pure' refugee camp."

"So things are stressed out?" I said.

"It is mostly Croatians who lost their homes to Serbs and a few Bosnians."

"Must suck for the Bosnians."

"It usually does," he said. He tore another piece of bread and dipped it in the soup. After he swallowed: "This Bosnian woman Marta has two children, Ruza and Ivan. Her husband is gone. He was Croatian, a Catholic. Who knows where? No one talks about him, but it's assumed he's dead. He hasn't been seen or heard from since the fall of '92. They lived in Foca when the Serbs took her husband. She was told the Red Cross in Jablanica would take care of her. She packed everything she could carry into two blue suitcases and got on a bus with Ruza and Ivan. But the Red Cross wasn't in Jablanica, no one was, just people who thought Bosnians were religious fanatics and murderers of Christians, you know?"

I put my hand to my chin, trying to give this serious contemplation.

He continued: "So she spent time in towns that didn't want her or her children. She lied about her name. She lied about her children being her children. And she eventually made it here, where she was also hated.

Because these people are all Croatians who fled an area that was overrun by Serbs who were pushed out of a town by Bosnians."

"Sounds crappy."

"But now there is a happy ending," and he turned to Gisela. "Marta got out. After writing letter after letter, she was eventually given an Austrian visa. The Croatian government let her leave."

"Cool."

"But the government decided, in all its wisdom, that the children were Croatian because the father was Croatian. Not Bosnian, so that they can't leave. The government needs Croatians to stay so there are people to populate the towns they take back from the Serbs.

"They can't move away with their mom, but a foreigner can sponsor them for a short time, for education or summer vacation. Things are different now. It's very easy. The government just needs to think they are coming back."

"Just for a short time?"

"Once they are out of the country, they can go anywhere. Gisela has offered to take them to Austria. To their mom. It will be simple."

❃ ❀ ❃

There wasn't a British consul in Rijeka, but at the tourist agency, I found a *Herald Tribune* that confirmed, a few pages in, a freelance journalist had been found in Knin. No one had claimed responsibility. Each side blamed the other, but there were no clear details. Only that he was the seventy-eighth journalist violently killed in the conflict.

❃ ❀ ❃

"Ruza understands English. She's very bright. Aren't you, Ruza?"

The girl didn't answer. She put her hands in her pockets and turned the inside of her elbows towards us and shrugged. The boy, Ivan, fingered a piece of smooth blue and green sea glass.

Between them, they had one small canvas bag and lunch packed in a paper sack. The boy held a milk bag filled with water and tied closed with a rubber band. They had been cleaned up since the day before and I felt some pride in them. I couldn't get over how little Ivan was. His little hands and quick movements lightened my anxiety.

I left a note for Marsh at the front desk, apologizing for leaving him, as if I could redirect reality. Maybe there was some dual universe, and maybe he was glad I'd left and he got a lot more done with me not there to sandbag his efforts. It couldn't hurt.

I went to retrieve the Trabant while Thomas and Gisela waited with the children in front of the hotel. I pulled up and had this kind of warm wholesome feeling, like we were going on a family outing, apple picking or a ball game. They both wanted to sit in back. Before they got in, the woman gave them each a hug and had a small talk with each one, looking them in the eye, hugging, kissing, and crying, then finally let them in the car.

"This is going to be fine," Thomas said to us. He gave us an address and number in Vienna and said Marta was registered with the Red Cross, and to go to them if there was any trouble.

"I'm not worried."

"You will be in Austria this time tomorrow."

"I know."

"I wouldn't ask you to help if we weren't desperate. You're good people. This is not a favor to me, this is for a helpless family."

"Yeah, of course."

Once everyone was in, and we were on the road, they looked so timid and sweet. I smiled at Gisela. She smiled back but her expression was sickly. She'd put on more makeup that morning than ever before and it highlighted hairs on her top lip that I'd never noticed.

At Thomas's suggestion, we drove up along the Istral Peninsula toward Trieste and then cut north into Slovenia. Darkness fell before we reached Ljubljana, and it began to softly rain. From the highway the sky was a greenish yellow where the city lights reached into the cloudy night sky. I was terrified of stopping. I felt untethered, so out of the world, in orbit with these two little helpless moons. At that point, Ruza, who allegedly spoke English, still hadn't answered any of our questions. I wouldn't even know where to begin if I was to have to explain them to anyone.

Thomas had given us some flimsy passports. They seemed comical but worked getting through the Croatian–Slovenian border. The guards looked at my passport with more interest than the children's.

They asked, "Hungary? Hungary?" a few times.

"*Egen, egen*. Hungary," Gisela promised.

They let us through.

At a rest stop on the highway in Slovenia, I bought an espresso, a postcard showing the rest stop, and an international postage stamp while Ruza took her brother into the bathroom. I quickly scribbled, "*Why aren't you here?*" and addressed it to Claire on Folsom Street and slipped it in the mail slot, unsigned.

For about one hundred kilometers, we were in Austria. The gas stations were newer. The roads were in better condition. We were closer to Vienna than we were to Budapest. Gisela was in and out of sleep. I was tempted to continue north.

We arrived at the Hungarian border around 5:00 AM. They took a few minutes leafing through our passports and the sponsorship documents, which looked like they were put together by the children themselves. The guards seemed baffled. They had us pull over while they called someone. Gisela became flirty. Both of the guards put on an earnest face when she spoke. The children slept through the questioning and having a flashlight repeatedly shined in their faces.

After ten minutes the guards got a call back and waved us on. I'm assuming no one wanted to deal because it was 5:00 AM.

By seven, the day was strongly on us. We were driving east and I had trouble seeing through the rising sun. I pulled over to shut my eyes for a few minutes, but the car quickly heated up, and Gisela asked me to keep going.

I had given Ivan and Ruza my blue REI bag; during the night they created a cocoon with it in the backseat. They had begun to unravel from the bag and their pink arms and faces were now peeking out, their flesh damp and sunburned, their cheeks and lips chubby with sleep. Their eyes twitched as they dreamt. Occasionally one of them murmured or cried out, then shook and settled. The car was ripe. The edges of the wind-shield foggy. It was soothing to finally see—when they rose from the horizon, came and went—the Hungarian road signs.

The road was empty for most of the morning. Telephone poles falling away were the only constant on the horizon. The rain, which stopped just before dawn, left the wet soil black as used coffee grains. Wisps of mist rose from the passing fields and wet tar. Lone farmhouses popped up every twenty kilometers or so. They were white concrete with red ceramic tile roofs. Water poured from the drain spouts into wooden barrels. White gates kept back small ratty dogs. Near the houses there were tracks of tomatoes and fields of green beans. Vines climbed yarn strung between ten-foot-high wooden poles. String beans the size of fingers weighed heavy on the vines. Fields of corn and grains further away from the houses made the low surrounding hills look wrapped in patchwork. Tractors stood abandoned from the day before in random spots on the fields, waiting for the farmers to climb back in and continue. By noon, we were in Budapest.

{fifteen}

THE MIDDAY STREETS were empty and noiseless. The air, warm and still. We had only been gone for eight days, but Budapest had changed. It was August. The heat was soft and worn. Summer was a sink full of dirty dishes. People were tired of it, they wanted to get serious again. They had spent all their money on trips to Balaton. Women were exhausted from the consciousness it took to wear summer dresses. Men wanted to let out their guts. People were sick of gelato. You could smell the Danube. Ruza and Ivan watched me as I gathered our stuff from the trunk.

I asked the girl how she was doing. She stared into me. "It's going to be okay," I said. "You're going to see your mom. It's going to be okay."

The old woman watched us from her window.

❊ ❊ ❊

In the morning, Ivan started crying. We gave him some yogurt. He spit it out. He still hadn't spoken. I thought I had heard that bawling was how babies exercised, but he was at least three. I looked to Ruza for help. She tried to pat him on the head. He started screaming, like how your average adult would scream if they were thrown from a plane. We gave him bread and some chocolate. We gave him ice. I walked him into the bathroom. I turned on the radio. I played Yo-Yo Ma. I shook a newspaper in front of him. I tried to hug him. I tried to give him a piggyback ride. We spoke slowly and quietly to him. We spoke loudly. I shook him gently. His whole body bristled to get away from me. We waited for his throat to go hoarse. We waited for a blood vessel in his temple to burst.

After three hours of on-and-off screaming, Gisela went down the hall and found the teenager who wore the tight corduroys and got her to babysit.

Picasso Point looked cheap and watered-down in the daylight. The plants were covered in a waxy gray film from cigarette smoke. Our table was pocked with cigarette burns and ringed stains from pints glasses. The sunlight came weakly through the windows.

"The tickets and papers should be here by Wednesday," she said.

"The little one, he doesn't look so smart," I said.

"He's just freaked out."

"Why scream your head off when people are giving you food? And doesn't it seem like he's got kind of a weird look on his face?"

"He's scared."

"Will they take him if he's mentally disabled?"

"Your parents took you."

"Maybe we should bring them to Vienna?"

"You think their mom can help them?" she asked, suddenly serious. "The sex trade. Austrian skinheads, the Russians. I don't even want to think about it. We are going to give them the most amazing life. Dishwashers, college, rich Mormons."

"But if no one wants him, do you still get paid?"

"Anthony, just stop."

✧ ✧ ✧

She took Ruza to the zoo for the afternoon. She had read in the paper they were going to euthanize a rhinoceros. I was reading an *Atlantic Monthly* and Ivan had finally fallen asleep on the couch. I ran to the door afraid the knocks would wake him.

Babette was standing in the hallway. She was wearing bell-bottom jeans, a maroon sweater with a single tan band across her chest, and a thin suede coat.

"Anthony?" she asked hesitantly. She had always been so quiet; it struck me for the first time that her English had a British accent.

"Hey," I said.

"You're back?"

"We just got back."

"Is he here?" She put a hand on the frame and lifted herself on her tiptoes and tried to look over my right shoulder into the apartment.

"Well, he's not. Just me. Just I'm back."

"Oh." Her body shrank. She took her arm down from the door frame. She looked me in the eye. "Where is he?"

"He stayed. He wasn't finished."

"He said you were driving him."

"He found someone else."

"Who?"

"Do you want to come in?" I pulled the door fully open and stepped back. She hesitated then entered the apartment. She looked thinner. Her pants were low riders and when she took off her coat, her shirt lifted and I saw the tops of her panties. I went over and closed the French doors that led into the living room where Ivan had passed out.

"You want something to drink?"

"He sent a card," she said. "It said you were coming home."

She pulled a postcard from her coat pocket. It was a picture of the Meteor that they sold at the front desk. It had been taken years before, sometime in the seventies. The building was pale yellow. There was a horse-drawn carriage at the steps leading up to the entrance. All the people on the patio were tan with big hair. The men were wearing ascots and double-breasted blazers. The women wore bright, one-piece poly-ester dresses with thigh-length hemlines.

My Babette,

We shouldn't be long. I've just wired one story and in two days will have the second done and then we should be home. Anthony and his girl are behaving well. I think the sea calms them. I miss you like cherry trees miss the spring.

My Longest Hardest Love,
Marsh

"I have some bad news." I turned the postcard over, looked at the front one more time, then handed it back to her.

"News?"

"You haven't heard anything else from him?"

"This just came two days ago." She held up the card. "He's okay?"

"Yeah. I think so. I think he's fine." I opened the miniature fridge. "We've got water. And beer, and I think there's some red wine. Do you drink wine?"

"What do you mean, 'You think so'? Where is he? Didn't he come back with you? We have an engagement party in two weeks. I start at the Conservatory in September."

"Well, we kind of got separated. I had to come back early. He kind of decided to stay a little longer." If they were so engaged, why was he hitting on Gisela?

"Why? He told me you were driving him. He doesn't drive, you know?"

"Oh, yeah, I know. But he found someone else." I opened one of the large green Drehers and split it two ways. I pushed a glass across the table to her. "I think he had a different ride back. I had to get home and he had to do some more work."

"You left him there?"

I stood up and walked to her side of the table.

"Well, no. Not really. I got arrested. And well . . . it was really stupid, but well . . . I was in jail and well . . ."

"Did he get arrested? Is Marsh in jail?" She was becoming short of breath. I laid my hand on hers.

"No, no, he wasn't arrested, just me. I got arrested. It's okay." I patted her hand. "He wasn't even there. I just did something really dumb."

"He wasn't supposed to go, you know? He didn't need to go down there. He already has another job. In England. We're going to move to London as soon as he gets back."

"What are you going to do there?"

"Me?" She was starting to tear. "I'm at the Liszt Institute. I was going to continue study at the Royal Conservatory." She shook her hand from mine and nervously played some imaginary keys on the table. "Well, so . . . where is he? How's he getting home?"

"You must be really good. The Conservatory is really famous."

"What do you mean, 'he decided to stay'? How is he getting home?" Her voice was rising.

I took my hand from the table and put it on her shoulder. "I don't know. Maybe the train. He had money and knew interpreters, is what I'm saying. This might not be true. I'm not sure about this." She looked at me, incredulous. "If this doesn't work out, if you're in trouble, I can take care of you. You could come back to the U.S. with me. I could totally take care of you. I owe him that much."

"What are you talking about?"

"He might not be all right, is all I'm saying. I'm not totally sure. I haven't heard from him." I had her by both shoulders now. "But I can totally take care of you, if you need help."

"Where is he?" Raising her voice.

When I hugged her, she tried to break my hold. "I don't know." I was saying this into her ear, trying to pull her towards me. Her hair smelled like banana bread. Some of it caught on my tongue and I was afraid it might slice the corner of my mouth if she pulled away so I held her tighter. She was light like an empty grocery bag but her elbow was below my rib cage. When she stood up from the stool, I backed her against the wall. I tried to kiss her on the forehead and then the cheeks and maybe the mouth. I told her over and over I could take care of her. She said no, no, no. Her body was saying something different. It was pushing into me. I let my hands fall to her behind and lifted her a little and she didn't stop and her legs spread so I was in between. I was bulging against my pants. She was bawling but it seemed about something else. Or it seemed recuperative. Then it didn't. She shook her head trying to get away from my mouth. Her hands were on my shoulders pushing back and she straightened her legs so they weren't around me. She slipped from my grip and stepped away. There was crying behind me. I turned. Ivan had pulled open a door. Tears were streaking out the corners of his eyes. I stepped back from Babette. "I'm sorry. I'm . . . really sorry. But it was confusing, it was crazy down there." With one hand, she covered her mouth like she was going to throw up. Then she looked up and I heard the slap of her hand hitting my face before I felt my head ring from it. She pushed me back and grabbed her coat from the seat and ran past Ivan and down the front hallway out the door.

✦✦✦

There was an all-day concert on an island out by Siget, fifteen kilometers north of the city. I wanted to get out of the apartment. I was a little concerned Babette would return. And I thought it would be nice to take them. Gisela thought Ivan was confused enough and didn't want to be dragging them around a rock concert.

"You can drink here," she said. "If you have to."

"It's not about drinking. I want to see some Hungarian culture, before we go."

I went alone.

There is a story in Hungarian history similar to our George Washington crossing the Potomac. In Eger, two hours north of Budapest, there is a castle. In the fifteenth century, the Turks had taken over Budapest. They'd taken over Debrecen and Pécs. They'd beheaded forty thousand. Minarets were popping up everywhere. The last of the Hungarian army—mainly civilian and a good number of Serbians—was holed up in this castle, cut off and supplies dwindling. The seventy thousand Turks camped outside the castle for two months, then decided to move in. The walls of the castle began to crumble and Captain Dobo rallied the Hungarians, saying, "The power of walls is not in the stone, but in the souls of the defenders." The Turkish forces headed up the main ramp. They began to bludgeon down the castle gates. When the gates finally gave, a large fiery wheel came out and rolled down into the Turkish forces, spitting hot oil and flames as it rolled. The Hungarians came out in the wake of the flaming wheel and they made quick work of the surviving Turks. This is often cited as an example of the wiliness of Hungarians.

After the main concert acts, which included a Deep Purple cover band, a solo horn sounded from the highest point on the island. The sky

was darkening. People were still milling around. The horn was beautiful, soft, and lonely. People began gathering at the foot of the hill. Then
torches lit up and you could make out the dark outline of a twenty-
foot-high wooden cable wheel. Then it was on fire and the crowd oohed
and ahhed. The wheel was budged forward. They were going to roll it
down the hill. I didn't know the story of Captain Dobo at the time
and thought this was some sort of drunken mayhem. The wheel began
to roll down the hill towards the crowd. People cleared a path. A few
drunk guys waited until the last second and had to dive out of the way.
But by the time the wheel was halfway down the hill, the fire had blown
out. People booed. The smoking wheel rolled lamely into the river and
began floating away.

I got home at around ten in the morning. My things were in a pile
in front of Gisela's door. The door was locked. There was no note. There
was an envelope with five thousand forints (about fifty dollars) under my
canvas duffle bag. I waited. I went to see if the car was where we'd left it.
It wasn't. I went back up and smoked a few cigarettes on the doorstep.
I waited until three and then went over to American Express on Fedra
Utca. I called my mother. She cried and told me my grandmother had
died, and she had no way of getting in touch. She agreed to wire me five
hundred dollars. When I picked the money up, there was actually one
thousand dollars.

My original return ticket was for September. Gisela and I had
planned on leaving earlier and paying to have it changed or attempt to
get on stand-by—but fall was a cheaper time to depart and would give us
time if needed. It was now August. I got a room in a youth hostel. I stayed
away from the expat bars and put some signs up at ELTE University trying to get some English tutoring jobs. I walked by Gisela's apartment
once a day.

On the tram one afternoon, I ran into Todd Verlaine. His stubble now had some gray in it. His gaze was bleary and his teeth were tinged a slight green-gray color and seemed rounder, but his face was still distinct and handsome. I'm sure he didn't know where he knew me from, but I was carrying a collection of Richard Ford stories. He pointed at the book and said, "That dude's a scumbag; he tried to fuck my girlfriend in college." He asked me if I wanted to get a coffee. We went to a small bodega near Parliament and ordered beers and two coffees. He told me Linklater had blackballed him and made him out to be a pariah, and as a result financing had fallen through. The deal was done. Even if his movie got shot, Linklater would make sure it'd never get distribution. The jealous bastard couldn't stand the heat. "My movie was top-shelf shit. Genius. Artuad, Curtis, Korda, all those guys. I was next. Till Rick assfucked me."

I asked him if he was going home.

"I can't go anywhere," he said. "This was my chance, and fucking Rick that motherfucking fuck fucked me. He's turned everyone in Austin against me, that rat-assed bitch. All my friends, those smarmy uninteresting turds. I can't go back there. Budapest is my only home now, a place where I'm still a shuddering speck in the scheme of things. I'm still a little dusty piece of nothing, but I'm not the same little dusty piece of nothing."

"Maybe it's blown over."

"Nothing blows over. Not with someone like Linklater, that malicious bastard. You don't know him."

"His movies are pretty good. *Slacker* was funny. He seems to have a sense of humor."

"Oh, yeah, that's what he wants you to think, but he's evil incarnate. Fucking asshole."

His hands were shaking. He dragged furiously on his cigarette, then broke into a hacking cough for two or three minutes.

"Did you know Marsh Mathison?" I asked.

"That British dude? Dolphins fan? Always going off about mass graves."

"Yeah," I said.

"Yeah, I know him."

"I think he got killed."

"In Yugoslavia?"

"Yeah," I said.

"Harsh. He was cool."

"Yeah," I said.

He ordered another beer, but I declined.

"Have you ever fucked a Moldovian?" he asked.

"No, pretty sure, no."

"You should, dude. You totally should."

"I'll think about it," I said. Then I told him I had to go. I dropped some money on the table. I said I'd see him around and went back to the hostel. I watched some Germans play Ping-Pong for a hour or so and then walked over to American Express and changed my ticket to leave that week.

{sixteen}

On an Indian summer Saturday morning about six weeks later, I was waiting in line at the Taqueria Cancun when behind me I heard: *"Olyani mint az csirke?"* She was wearing a thin blue cotton halter-top with a dark short skirt, Doc Marten boots, and ironically zany knee-high socks. In Budapest, she had once brought me to the farmers' market in Obuda and when we saw a man selling frog's legs, she taught me the Hungarian for the phrase *tastes like chicken.*

"What do you want?" I asked.

"I was on the bus and saw you walking. I thought I'd say hi," she said.

"Hi," I said.

"What's wrong?" She looked into my eyes, trying to get me to smile.

"What do you want?" I asked.

"Nothing, just saying hello."

I was up. I ordered a Chicken Burrito Supreme.

"You owe me some money," I said when I finished.

"You need money?"

"No, you *owe* me money. You completely ditched me. I had no money and no way home."

"You're home now."

"I quit my job to go over there with you."

"You didn't have to do that. I didn't make you."

"You completely ditched me."

"You're the one who went off to the concert and left me with them."

"I was gone for a day, barely a day."

What would happen if I kicked her? Or stepped on her feet and pushed her backwards like kids used to do on the playground at St. Alphonsus?

"What are you doing now?" she asked.

"Temping. At the Bank of America."

"No, right now," she said.

"Lunch."

"You want to see something?"

"Like what?"

"My new job? It's funny. You would like it. I get to wear a silly dress."

I tried to look pissed.

She reached out and lightly brushed the back of her fingers against my forearm. "Come on, this is funny. It'll only take a few minutes." My burrito was ready. I followed her out.

❂ ❂ ❂

The electric buses wheezed and hissed down Mission. Wanna-be gang members, pool ball shoulders and teardrop tattoos, furious but acutely aware of the vast reserves of indifference the world possessed for them. A rotisserie slowly turning three prongs full of thin white chickens in the window of a Pollo Rey. Vendors selling *paletas* and *batidos*. Hairstylists and beauty shops with water-stained advertisements touting decade-old hairdos and Tammy-Faye-Bakker-thick makeovers. Gisela's ass doing that horsey thing. I wanted to climb inside it. But then we were in the no-man's land around 8th and Market and she turned down an alley to the small steel door of a warehouse. I followed her inside and up some metal stairs to the second floor loft.

There was one large room, a small alcove of a kitchen on one side, and a bathroom off the other. The main room was painted midnight blue and was nearly two stories high. A hide-away bed was tucked in halfway up the back wall. It was too high to reach from the ground. I couldn't see how one got to it.

She walked up behind me and asked if I wanted a drink. I said yes, but didn't turn around. I was waiting for something more. I heard her feet pad into the kitchen.

One wall was books. Mostly soft-covered, but a few ancient-looking green and brown ones with gold gilding. They were stacked tightly but in seemingly random order, back and forth, all the way up to the ceiling. At least two thousand of them. There were dictionaries in three or four languages. Hesse and the Tantra and a few books in Sanskrit. English words and staples jumped out at me like the faces of people in a photo taken long ago, a first-grade class photo: Fitzgerald, Conrad, Hemingway, Shakespeare, a few poetry anthologies, *Green Eggs and Ham*. And this relaxed me. Whoever's apartment this was, they understood there've been artists and writers who've existed and made things that now appear perfect, inevitable, and integral parts of humanity. Then I saw *Catch-22*. I yelled into the kitchen, asking if she'd read it.

"Ah. Yes, Anthony." She started speaking in Hungarian and I recognized *"huz en ketto,"* Hungarian for "twenty two."

"Do you know what it means?" I asked.

"Yes but no. Yes?"

"More or less."

I sat down in the soft leather sofa. Three deep glass aquariums held snakes that slept under dark lights, and next to them a smaller aquarium filled with sawdust and a bunch of rats that lived on top of each other. Five or six white bunnies were piled in a small metal cage. Occasionally one of them hopped.

Then she was in front of me. *"Kaffee?"*

"Kosenem saipen." We were pretending. I took the little white cup from her hand. And she slipped back into the kitchen.

A glass bowl of cheap caviar, a clump of lard, some crackers, four different glass carafes each containing a different-colored liquor, and four Marlboros. She laid the tray on the coffee table next to my burrito.

"Nice? No?"

"Yeah, *Remek.*"

"Remek?" She rolled her *r*'s when she said it. Her smile was dizzying.

"Who lives here?" I asked.

"Yes. *Remek.*" Again she exaggeratedly rolled her *r*'s.

"Who lives here?"

She said a few sentences in Hungarian which I didn't understand a word of. *"Igen?"* she asked.

"Whose apartment is this?"

"Caviar. Fish? You like, Anthony?"

It was probably close to 1:00 PM, but little light made it into the apartment. I looked around for pictures of the owner. A few ancient, yellowed black-and-whites were scattered on the walls. The tiny, sharp-featured, black-haired people in them were dressed in nineteenth-century garb. Hungarians from a time when Budapest was Vienna's sister. The two cities balancing the slightly feared Austro-Hungarian Empire. Many Hungarians still believe their country was one of two equals in this arrangement. They believe there was more to it than the Austrians using Hungary for its fertile prairies and cheap labor. But none of these handsome ancestors looked anything like the striking Gisela. And again I asked her whose apartment this was.

"*Es gute?* No?"

"*Wohnst du hier?*"

"*Nem.* No, Anthoneeey." And she laughed a phony "ha ha ha" as if I had said something incredibly naive. "*Mein Illusionist,*" she said.

"Illusionist?" I asked, but I'm thinking, pimp. Her pimp. A huge man named Zolt, part of some kind of international sex trade, a man who reads a lot and still has no respect whatsoever for women, people, human life in general. Someone who pays his rent with someone else's suffering, who'd have no problem cashing in on mine.

"Yes. Anthoneey. You know?"

"*Ich glaube, ich weiss nicht.*" I pictured the bed way up on the wall somehow used in an asphyxiation trick.

"Yes, *du wisst,*" she said. "*Er is ein Zauber. Ich helfe ihm.*" He is a *Zauber.* And I help him. *Zauber?* Sour? I could usually follow her German but I had no idea what she was saying. I was praying she'd gone prostitute. A long-legged, healthy woman who's more than comfortable with her face in a pillow and her behind raised to me like an offering. She wants to make up for treating me poorly.

"*Warten.*" And she walked over to a large cabinet. The doors slid apart and there was a VCR and brand-new Sony television. "I show you, Anthony." She pulled a videotape from the lower console. Porn, yes, yes, yes, international porn. Yes. She put the tape in and once it was going, hit one of the lights, and went back into the kitchen. I heard bottles and jars moving.

The tape was home-movie quality. It showed the downtown of a small farming town. It was dusk. There were pickup trucks lining the street and people were milling around, sitting on the back bumpers, looking in shop windows. Then the people began moving into a meeting hall. There was a sign over the foyer with black block lettering. The cameraman kept focusing unsuccessfully on the words, but there was a second when it seemed to read PARMA. Then the screen went dark and there was silence. I began to ask Gisela what was up, when it started again. We were being shown the inside of the meeting hall. Gypsy music played in the background and the volume increased and decreased as the camera swept from one thing to another. The seats were filling up. Then the lights went out. The stage lit up. A man stuck his head out between the curtains, looked around, then disappeared. A few seconds later, the curtain parted.

The man stood in the spotlight wearing a tuxedo and holding a golf club. He was speaking English with a Hungarian accent. He welcomed the crowd and introduced himself as Houdini's great-nephew. He pulled out a golf ball and bounced it a few times, making loud cracks when the ball met the wooden stage. Then he bent down and placed the ball on a small patch of artificial turf that you didn't notice until he placed the ball on it. He swung the club like someone who knew how to play, drilling the ball into the audience. People screamed. The camera scanned the crowd. The spotlight switched from the stage to an area in the middle. People cowered under their chairs. Men in cowboy shirts were low, ducking while trying to exit their rows. You expected to see an elderly woman clutching an eye. But then the magician started yelling, pleading for them to stay. Then there was laughter. Somehow the ball never hit the audience, or the ball disappeared, or he aimed it perfectly into a glove held by someone planted in the audience. You couldn't tell. Abracadabra. After some more talk and laughter, he pulled a pigeon out of thin air. Before sticking it in his pocket, he leaned down like he was going to place the bird on the tee as well. The audience ate it up. The music quickened. Gisela walked out onto the stage. She wore a tutu and held a bowl of goldfish. She handed him the bowl, turned, and exited the stage. He took the bowl up to his lips like a chalice and began to drink. After the water was gone, he reached in and plucked the goldfish out one by one and ate them. The final fish were difficult and at one point he looked up and burped. He said *scusa* then went back to concentrating on the fish, like he was getting the last few chips from the bag. He finished them, then hucked the empty goldfish bowl into the audience. Again, shrieks and gasps, but the bowl never landed. It disappeared somewhere over the audience members' heads.

Gisela again appeared. This time she had a cigar case. She presented him with the open case. He selected a cigar, pulled a small set of scissors from his coat, clipped off the ends. She presented him with a flame. He pulled on the cigar until we could see the burning ember. He then looked at Gisela like he had just thought of something and held up his finger telling her to wait. He dragged on the cigar and made like he was going to whisper into her ear. He leaned over and cupped his hand around her ear, and like he only now realized he had a mouth full of smoke, he looked up, exacerbated, and exhaled, blowing the smoke in one ear and out the other. The audience erupted. When Gisela shook her head and stuck a finger in the ear, more smoke exited. Then she started to yell at the magician and smoke billowed from her mouth. She exited the stage in frustration and the magician ate the rest of the cigar. Sparks and cigar bits dribbled from his mouth as he slowly and messily chewed.

Gisela appeared again. She rolled out a black trunk with metal edges. An audience member was invited up to inspect it. He nodded to his fellow audience members that it is a trunk. Gisela climbed in. She wiggled her head and feet out from the ends. The magician pulled a saw from a sheaf and brandished it in the air. He sawed her in half. Then thirds. Then he pushed her back together. Her feet wiggled. She pretended to burp. Small trails of smoke leaked from her mouth. The magician acted disgusted and threw a black sheet over her and the trunk. She made peeping noises, protesting her predicament. He removed the sheet, but she was gone.

The lights in the apartment went on and she was standing next to me in the tutu. We continued drinking the illusionist's liquors. She showed me pictures of Ivan, Ruza, and an ecstatic woman standing on the steps of a massive opera house. The signs were in German. She had brought them back to their mother. At some point her head was in my lap and I was thinking that she'd be different now that we were back in San Francisco. We had shared so much. I wasn't dependent on her here.

Two days later we were in Doc's Clocks after dinner and she began talking to a guy I recognized from the Bank of America mailroom as a bike messenger. At last call, she told me she wanted to be alone that night.

{seventeen}

I HAVE THE TAPES I TOOK from his bag. With the exception of one, they're dated from before I knew him. And none of it is really interesting. One has a funny monologue where he rails against dogs and cats, saying domestic animals are a direct result of the automobile because once horses weren't needed there was an excess of horsemeat and for the first time in the history of the world the hoi polloi could afford carnivorous pets. But the rest are about the war. I get drunk on Bull's Blood, which you can buy by the case at Trader Joe's, and sit on the back steps of my basement apartment and listen to them. He's talking hesitantly—you can hear him smoking—nesting little shreds of thought and observation into stories. But also, he sounds embarrassed. *More dead, I think seventeen. Call Elba. May 15th, the Red Cross is being kept away. "Dimije" are what the Muslims call their baggy trousers. People get shot for wearing them. I don't trust the driver. It was odd last night. That Drago person, his English was poor but he kept using the phrase "survive the winter." Where'd he learn it? This American? For them the future is a speck on the horizon, and instead of chasing it, they seem content letting it come to them.*

And one day I got a letter from his mother. It had been sent to my parents in Skaneateles, and then forwarded by my mother. My note had been found on his body. Her letter is penned in sepia ink. *I don't need answers,* she writes. *Just let me know something. He told me of a friend with a Roman nose. Is that you? Was he happy? Could we meet for cake?*

{acknowledgments}

Charlie, Owen, Emilee, Margaret and Michael Sr., Randi Davenport, David Bajo, Seth Factor, Ted Grennan, James McDermott, Mark Lane, Rich Wandschneider and Fishtrap, the Idaho Commission on the Arts, James Brownrigg Dillard II, Diana Finch, Jane Vandenburgh, Jack Shoemaker, Trish Hoard, Roxanna Font, and all the amazing people at Shoemaker & Hoard. I'm so incredibly lucky and grateful. Thank you.

PHOTO BY MARK JONES

MICHAEL A. FITZGERALD lives in Idaho with his wife and his two young sons. He holds an MFA from the University of Montana. This is his first novel.